62 Easy and Delicious Cooking Activities

Jean Bunnell

illustrated by Lafe Locke

J. Weston Walch, Publisher
Portland, Maine

REPRODUCTION OF COPY MASTERS

These copy masters are designed for individual student use and intended for reproduction by dry copier, liquid duplicating machine, or other means.

J. Weston Walch, Publisher, therefore transfers limited reproduction rights to the purchaser of these masters at the time of sale. These rights are granted only to a single classroom teacher, whether that teacher is the purchaser or the employee of a purchasing agent such as a school district. The masters may be reproduced in quantities sufficient for individual use by students under that teacher's direct classroom supervision.

Reproduction of these masters for use by other teachers or students is expressly prohibited and constitutes a violation of United States Copyright Law.

2   3   4   5   6   7   8   9   10

ISBN 0-8251-1117-X

Copyright © 1987
J. Weston Walch, Publisher
P.O. Box 658 • Portland, Maine 04104-0658

Printed in the United States of America

CONTENTS

(Note: Recipes in this set are arranged alphabetically.)

Introduction	v
Overview of Recipes	vii
Teacher Notes	ix
How to Play NUTRO	xxix

MASTERS

NUTRO—The game with food for thought	1
Amazing Soup	2
Ambrosia	3
Apple Turnover	4
Beef Stroganoff	6
Beverages (4 Recipes)	8
Breakfast Pizza	10
Butter-Crumb Vegetables	11
Butterscotch Biscuits	13
Carrot-Potato Cake	14
Cheddar Cheese Crackers	15
Cheese Dog	16
Cheese Soup	17
Chicken Noodle Soup	18
Chili	20
Chow Mein	21
Corn Chowder	23
Crepes	24
Dilly Dippers	26
Egg Foo Yung	28
Four-Square Tortilla	30
Fruit Cones	31
Fruit Kabob	33
Ham Roll-Up	34
Muffin Sampler (5 Recipes)	35
Omelet	38
Peanut Butter Soup	39
Peanut Crunchies	41

Pretzels	**42**
Rice Variations	**44**
Sausage and Pepper Hero	**47**
Scones & Strawberry Jam	**49**
Snow Ice Cream	**50**
Stuffed Pasta Shells	**51**
Stuffed Pita Pockets	**52**
Sweet & Sour Meatballs	**54**
Tomato Flower	**56**
Tomato Soup	**58**
Tossed Salad	**59**
Tuna Cheesie	**60**
Vegetable Bouquet	**61**
Vegetable Sampler (3 Recipes)	**63**
Waldorf Salad	**65**
Walnut Chicken & Rice	**66**
Welsh Rarebit	**68**

62 Easy and Delicious Cooking Activities

INTRODUCTION

62 Easy and Delicious Cooking Activities contains a selection of recipes to entice young people into the kitchen and equip them with the ability to transform what they find into something edible and nutritious. Traditional kid-pleasing recipes are included along with a variety of appetizing foreign foods as well as standard offerings and variations-on-a-theme. Each recipe can be completed in a single class period.

Most kids like to cook! Cooking provides an opportunity to create and to be successful. From a sandwich to a classic main dish; from breakfast to dessert —all of these recipes have been chosen because kids will be able to prepare them quickly and easily. They will be pleased and impressed with what they have accomplished. *62 Easy and Delicious Cooking Activities* will help students develop the confidence to cook on their own.

Nutrition is a consideration throughout. Recipes use a wide variety of easily-available ingredients. Students preparing the recipes will become familiar with basic kitchen skills and equipment.

Each recipe is written in an easy-to-follow format and is designed for maximum student involvement. Nearly half the recipes are for individual servings, enabling each student to make the entire product from start to finish. Many recipes are suited for groups of 4 students to prepare. Some recipes can be larger projects — with as many as 12 or more students working cooperatively. The Overview of Recipes chart shows how the recipes are organized. The amount of food prepared in each recipe provides a sample for each student involved in the preparation.

In recipes where students work together, a line has been provided before each step of the preparation. This is to help students in their planning. Each blank can be used for recording the name of the person who will complete that particular step.

Graphics on the masters help make instructions clear. Many of the worksheets include bonus activities which the teachers and students can choose to use or not as they please. The accompanying Teacher Notes include shopping lists and helpful comments about each project.

Overview of Recipes

Type of Recipe	Recipes for Individual Servings	Recipes for Small Groups (four)	Recipes for Large Groups (twelve)
Vegetables	Carrot-Potato Cake Tomato Flower Vegetable Bouquet	Butter-Crumb Vegetables Dilly Dippers Vegetable Sampler	Tossed Salad
Soups	Cheese Soup Tomato Soup	Chicken Noodle Soup Corn Chowder Peanut Butter Soup	Amazing Soup
Main Dishes	Cheese Dog Four-Square Tortilla Ham Roll-up Tuna Cheesie	Beef Stroganoff Chili Stuffed Pasta Shells Stuffed Pita Pockets Sweet & Sour Meatballs Walnut Chicken & Rice	Chow Mein Sausage & Pepper Hero
Desserts/Snacks	Apple Turnover Beverages Snow Ice Cream	Crepes Peanut Crunchies	
Eggs/Cheese	Breakfast Pizza Omelet Welsh Rarebit	Egg Foo Yung	
Fruit	Fruit Kabob Waldorf Salad	Ambrosia	Fruit Cones
Bread/Rice	Cheddar Cheese Crackers Rice Variations	Butterscotch Biscuits Muffin Sampler Pretzels Scones & Strawberry Jam	

Note: Recipes in this set are arranged alphabetically.

Teacher Notes

Amazing Soup

Objectives: 1. Use canned vegetables to make a quick soup.
2. Combine "on-hand" ingredients for soup.

Notes: This "recipe" is a variation on the popular camping "Stone Soup." Anything works!

If desired, have students each bring a can of vegetables from home for this project. Seasonings can be changed as desired. Add a pinch of garlic powder or dill or oregano. This recipe can be expanded for any number. You might want to add a little more meat, soup and herbs. The basic guide is one can of vegetables per person. To cut down on salt content, you may choose to have students drain the cans of vegetables. Replace liquid with equal amount of unsalted tomato juice.

Shopping list for 12 students (working as one group):

1 pound ground beef
one 10-ounce can condensed cream of celery soup
2 teaspoons dried parsley
12 small cans (4 to 6 ounces) of a variety of vegetables

Ambrosia

Objectives: 1. Prepare a dessert with attention to attractiveness.
2. Develop skill in preparing fruit.

Notes: If Valencia oranges are unavailable, another kind can be substituted. Be sure any seeds are removed. The bonus activity suggests how a fresh coconut can be used.

Shopping list for 12 students (3 groups):

6 Valencia oranges
6 bananas
1½ pineapples
3 cups shredded coconut
¾ cup confectioners' sugar

Optional: fresh coconut

Apple Turnover

Objectives: 1. Demystify pastry making.
2. Prepare a dessert pastry.

Notes: Any variety of fillings can be used for this recipe. Apples are easy and convenient for individual turnovers, but a date or raisin filling could also be made for all members of the groups to use.

One trick for sprinkling confectioners' sugar on turnovers is to put it in a sifter or strainer. Then hold the sugar over the turnovers and give a quick push on it for a fine, even sprinkling.

Shopping list for 12 students (working individually):

3 cups flour (plus flour for rolling out dough)
salt (not more than 2 teaspoons)
¾ cup vegetable shortening
6 apples
¾ cup sugar
1 tablespoon cinnamon
confectioners' sugar for dusting (not more than 2 tablespoons)

Beef Stroganoff

Objectives: 1. Prepare a classic main dish.
2. Cook noodles.

Notes: This is a recipe that students can certainly use at home to prepare for their families. Other cuts of meat can be substituted. The less expensive chuck steak could be used.

Shopping list for 12 students (3 groups):

1½ pounds fine egg noodles
3 pounds beef tenderloin
3 medium onions
¾ pound fresh mushrooms
6 tablespoons butter or margarine
1 tablespoon dry mustard
black pepper (not more than ½ teaspoon)
three 10½-ounce cans cream of mushroom soup
1½ cups sour cream

Beverages (4 Recipes)

Objectives: 1. Prepare a refreshing beverage.
2. Compare a variety of easy-to-prepare drinks.

Notes: Four recipes are included on this page. Each recipe makes one drink. You may choose to have extra ingredients on hand and simply have each student select whichever recipe he or she would like to prepare.

Another approach might be to divide students into groups of four, with each student in a group preparing a different beverage. Students could divide the drink they prepare into 4 small paper cups. Then members of each group could sample all 4 recipes.

Shopping list for 12 students (assuming each recipe made by 3 students):

3 small ripe bananas
4½ cups milk
1½ teaspoons almond flavoring
nutmeg (not more than one teaspoon)
3 oranges
1½ cups ginger ale or club soda
3 small eggs
3 teaspoons vanilla extract
¾ cantaloupe
1½ cups apple juice
crushed ice (approximately 1½ to 2 cups)

Breakfast Pizza

Objectives: 1. Cook eggs.
2. Prepare a pizza variation for the breakfast table.

Notes: Breakfast is a meal that many teenagers (as well as adults) often skip. This combination of favorite flavors may entice some to this meal. The recipe is designed for students to each prepare individual servings.

Shopping list for 12 students (working individually):

6 English muffins
12 slices bacon
1 dozen eggs
1½ cups spaghetti sauce
¼ cup grated Parmesan cheese

Butter-Crumb Vegetables

Objectives: 1. Prepare raw vegetables for cooking.
2. Serve vegetables in an appealing variation.

Notes: Vegetables are often low on students' lists of preferred foods. Learning to cook them correctly and interestingly may help make them more appealing.

A ½ teaspoon garlic powder can be substituted for the garlic clove if preferred.

Shopping list for 12 students (3 groups):

    3 small heads of cauliflower (or 1 large one divided)
    ¾ head red cabbage
    9 medium carrots
    4½ cups bok choy greens (approximately 2 small heads)
    6 tablespoons butter or margarine
    3 cloves garlic
    12 slices whole grain bread
    black pepper (not more than 1½ teaspoons)

Butterscotch Biscuits

Objective: Develop skill in preparing biscuit dough.

Notes: The basic recipe is for standard "baking powder biscuits." It is a recipe which almost anyone will have a variety of occasions to use.

Shopping list for 12 students (3 groups):

    1½ cups flour (plus flour for rolling out dough)
    3-¾ teaspoons baking powder
    ¾ teaspoon sugar
    4½ tablespoons margarine or butter
    ¾ cup milk
    3 tablespoons brown sugar

Carrot-Potato Cake

Objective: Prepare potatoes in a new way.

Notes: Potatoes are enjoying a bit of good press. People are discovering that potatoes are a healthy food and should be a part of our diet. If cooking in butter is a problem because of scorching, try using half butter and half oil. The butter gives a good flavor.

Shopping list for 12 students (working individually):

    12 medium potatoes
    12 medium carrots
    3 small onions
    ¾ cup butter or margarine
    salt (not more than a tablespoon)

Cheddar Cheese Crackers

Objectives:
1. Make an unleavened cracker.
2. Use grated cheese for a flavor addition.

Notes: This recipe calls for 1 teaspoon of egg yolk. One egg yolk will provide enough for 2 or 3 students. Separating the eggs ahead will facilitate classroom procedure.

Shopping list for 12 students (working individually):

    3 cups flour (plus flour for rolling out dough)
    1 tablespoon salt
    ground ginger (not more than 1½ teaspoons)
    sugar (not more than a tablespoon)
    3 cups grated cheddar cheese (about 12 ounces)
    ¾ cup butter or margarine
    6 eggs (approximately — needed for yolks only)
    ¾ cup toasted sesame seeds

Cheese Dog

Objective: Prepare the traditional hot dog in a new way.

Notes: All the hot dogs can be cooked together on one pan after the students have stuffed and wrapped them. Students will get very involved in devising ways to distinguish their hot dog from the others on the pan after they are cooked!

Shopping list for 12 students (working individually):

    12 hot dogs
    12 slices American cheese
    12 slices bacon
    12 hot dog buns

Cheese Soup

Objective: Prepare a classic soup.

Notes: Cooking goes most easily if all ingredients are prepared and measured ahead of time. This is certainly a recipe to reinforce that concept! Once the butter is melted, total attention is needed to prepare the soup. There is no time to grate cheese or cook toast as they are called for in the recipe.

Shopping list for 12 students (working individually):

> 6 small onions
> 4 cups shredded Swiss Cheese (about 18 ounces)
> 6 slices pumpernickel bread
> ¾ cup butter or margarine
> ¾ cup flour
> 3 quarts milk
> 4 tablespoons chopped parsley

Chicken Noodle Soup

Objectives: 1. Use a new kind of noodle for soup.
2. Cook chicken.

Notes: Cellophane noodles are an interesting alternative to pasta or rice in this soup recipe.

> If desired, the chicken can be cooked ahead for even shorter preparation time in the classroom.

Shopping list for 12 students (3 groups):

> 1½ chicken breasts
> 3 bunches cellophane noodles (about 3 ounces)
> 6 scallions
> 2 tablespoons soy sauce
> pepper (not more than ¼ teaspoon)

Chili

Objectives: 1. Prepare a popular main dish.
2. Use seasonings.

Notes: Ground beef is a favorite! Any recipe with ground beef will probably appeal to teenagers.

> Chili powder may be new to some students and should be used with caution so that the dish is not too spicy for those not used to hot foods. Garlic powder (½ teaspoon) can be substituted for the garlic clove if desired.

Shopping list for 12 students (3 groups):

> 3 small onions
> 3 medium cloves of garlic
> 3 tablespoons butter or margarine
> 1½ pounds ground beef

1½ green peppers
1 tablespoon chili powder
¾ teaspoon basil
3 cups tomatoes
3 cups kidney beans

Chow Mein

Objectives:
1. Cook an oriental main dish.
2. Prepare a variety of vegetables for cooking.
3. Trim and cut pork for cooking.

Notes: Chinese noodles make this a crunchy dish. If you prefer, rice can be used instead.

This mixture can be made in a large frying pan, a Dutch oven, or in a wok.

The recipe lends itself to preparation by a large group. Working singly or in pairs, students can prepare the meat, the vegetables, the sauce, and the noodles. It can then all be assembled quickly with each student (or pair of students) adding what they have prepared.

Shopping list for 12 students (working as 1 group):

1 pound pork steak
1 large onion
6 stalks celery
½ large green pepper
¼ pound mushrooms
8-ounce can water chestnuts
1-pound can bean sprouts
3 tablespoons cooking oil
1½ tablespoons cornstarch
1½ tablespoons soy sauce
5-ounce can Chinese noodles

Corn Chowder

Objective: Prepare a main-dish soup.

Notes: Bacon is not essential for this recipe. If it is preferred, skip the bacon. Melt 2 tablespoons of butter or margarine to use instead of bacon fat. Proceed with cooking the onion.

Shopping list for 12 students (3 groups):

12 slices bacon
3 small onions

6 medium potatoes
3 cups cream-style corn
pepper (not more than ½ teaspoon)
1½ cups half-and-half

Crepes

Objective: Prepare an elegant dessert.

Notes: A group of 4 students can work together to prepare the batter. Each student then can take a turn cooking and filling his or her own crepe.

Shopping list for 12 students (3 groups):

2¼ cups flour
1½ tablespoons sugar
¾ teaspoon baking powder
¾ teaspoon salt
3 cups milk
3 eggs
¾ teaspoon vanilla
3 tablespoons margarine
1½ cups strawberry jam (approximately)
confectioners' sugar (not more than ½ cup)

Dilly Dippers

Objectives:
1. Make a dip to serve with vegetables.
2. Prepare raw vegetables to serve with a dip.

Notes: This recipe has been reduced to allow maximum student involvement. If anyone wanted to make this dip to serve a larger number of people, it could easily be increased. A large round loaf of bread could be used for serving the dip.

Shopping list for 12 students (3 groups):

6 large carrots
6 stalks of celery
3 cucumbers
1 cup sour cream
3 tablespoons mayonnaise
1½ teaspoons minced onion (fresh or dehydrated)
1½ teaspoons dill weed
1½ teaspoons seasoned salt
1 tablespoon dried parsley
3 bulky rolls

Egg Foo Yung

Objective: Prepare an egg dish.

Notes: This is another recipe that can be great for using leftovers. Use different meat or add other vegetables if desired.

Students can work together in groups to prepare batter. Then each student can cook his or her own individual serving.

Shopping list for 12 students (3 groups):

   1 dozen eggs
   6 green onions
   3 tablespoons soy sauce
   6 stalks celery
   ¾ green pepper
   3 cups bean sprouts
   three 4½-ounce cans tiny shrimp
   4 tablespoons cooking oil

Four-Square Tortilla

Objectives:
1. Use a tortilla as bread for a sandwich.
2. Prepare a sandwich with foods from all 4 food groups.

Notes: Tortillas are best if they are warmed ahead. The directions are given for heating them in the oven. If desired, all of these can be heated together and then distributed for individual students to fill.

Shopping list for 12 students (working individually):

   12 tortillas
   4 tablespoons mayonnaise
   12 slices ham or salami
   12 slices cheese
   1 head lettuce
   6 carrots
   3 cups alfalfa sprouts

Fruit Cones

Objectives:
1. Prepare a variety of fruits for serving.
2. Use ice cream cones in a new way.

Notes: There is no recipe for fruit salad — any fruit can be added in any amount according to the preference of the person in charge! This recipe is designed to provide an activity for each of 12 students. Ten students can each prepare 1 of the 10 fruits; one student can mix the dressing; one can chop the nuts. When the fruit is mixed together and drained, each student can fill his or her own cone.

Before putting the fruit in the cones, it is important to drain the salad well so the cones will not turn to instant mush!

Shopping list for 12 students (working as one group):

> 1 dozen ice cream cones (sugar)
> 1 cantaloupe
> 2 oranges
> ½ pound seedless grapes
> 2 bananas
> 2 apples
> 2 pears
> 2 peaches
> 1 pint strawberries
> 1 grapefruit
> ½ pineapple
> ¾ cup dairy sour cream
> 2 tablespoons honey
> 2 tablespoons orange juice concentrate
> ½ cup walnuts

Fruit Kabob

Objectives:
1. Serve fruit in a new way.
2. Practice preparing fruit for serving.

Notes: A large variety of fruit can be used with this recipe, but be sure the fruits you choose are not ones that could be discolored in the air (i.e., banana or apple).

Wooden kabob sticks are usually available in grocery stores in packages of 50 to 100.

Shopping list for 12 students (working individually):

> 3 of the following fruits:
> > 1 cantaloupe
> > 2 quarts strawberries
> > 1 pound grapes
> > 1½ pounds watermelon (about three 1-inch slices of a halved watermelon)
> > 6 peaches
> > 6 pears
>
> 12 wooden kabob sticks

Ham Roll-Up

Objective: Use refrigerator rolls to make a sandwich.

Notes: Refrigerator rolls can be used in a variety of ways. Having them available eliminates mixing the dough and makes food preparation even simpler.

Shopping list for 12 students (working individually):

    1 dozen frozen refrigerator crescent rolls
    12 slices ham
    12 slices American cheese
    4 tablespoons mustard

Muffin Sampler (5 Recipes)

Objectives:
1. Make muffins.
2. Adapt a recipe to suit individual tastes.

Notes: Each group can make a different kind of muffin. Break each muffin into pieces and have a "muffin-tasting" party!

Shopping list for 12 students (3 groups and materials for one variation per group):

    3 small eggs
    6 tablespoons salad oil
    ¾ cup milk
    2¼ cups flour
    ¾ cup sugar
    1 tablespoon baking powder
    ⅜ teaspoon salt
    1 apple
    1 teaspoon cinnamon
    2 tablespoons brown sugar
    ½ cup fresh blueberries
    4 teaspoons jelly or jam
    1 orange

Omelet

Objectives:
1. Select ingredients for an omelet filling.
2. Cook eggs.

Notes: Almost any kitchen has a few eggs and some leftovers in the fridge. That is all that is needed for an omelet. So knowing how to make an omelet can be a real survival skill.

Adaptability is the secret of success with an omelet. Any number of fillings will work, depending on the taste preferences of the cook and the ingredients available!

Shopping list for 12 students (working individually):

> 2 dozen eggs
> ¾ cup butter or margarine
> fillings—have available some of the following:
> > cheese
> > tomatoes
> > meat (cooked chicken or other leftover)
> > green pepper
> > onion
> > other vegetables
>
> salt (not more than 1½ teaspoons)
> pepper (not more than 1 teaspoon)
> 12 sprigs of parsley

Peanut Butter Soup

Objectives:
1. Make a new soup with a traditional flavor.
2. Use peanut butter in a new way.

Notes: Peanut butter is standard fare for many teenagers. This recipe offers a new way to serve it!

Use creamy peanut butter, not chunky.

Shopping list for 12 students (3 groups):

> 3 small onions
> ¾ cup butter or margarine
> 3 tablespoons flour
> 1½ cups peanut butter
> 6 chicken boullion cubes
> salt (not more than ½ teaspoon)
> pepper (not more than ¼ teaspoon)
> 1½ cups light cream
> 6 tablespoons peanuts

Peanut Crunchies

Objectives: Make a nutty snack.

Notes: Sweets are always a favorite. This recipe combines the sugar with the nutrition-filled peanut.

Shopping list for 12 students (3 groups):

> 1½ pounds (approximately) unsalted peanuts in the shell
> 1 cup sugar
> 1½ teaspoons cinnamon

Pretzels

Objectives:
1. Make a bread variation.
2. Use yeast.

Notes: Students will each be able to shape their own pretzel. They can make the traditional shape, a letter of the alphabet, or any design they choose.

If there is more time, shaped pretzels can be left to rise for half an hour before baking, but it is not absolutely essential for a satisfactory result.

Shopping list for 12 students (3 groups):

1½ tablespoons yeast (1 tablespoon yeast in each envelope)
6 cups flour
1½ tablespoons sugar
margarine to grease baking sheet (1-2 tablespoons)
3 eggs
coarse salt (kosher salt can be purchased at specialty stores)

Rice Variations (7 Recipes)

Objectives:
1. Prepare rice.
2. Use imagination to make rice variations.

Notes: This recipe makes individual servings of rice. Each student can prepare a different variation and then share the results.

This recipe gives students a chance to be creative in planning a variety of ways to serve rice.

Shopping list for 12 students (working individually, 2 students preparing each variation):

3 cups regular white rice
1 tablespoon salt
2 beef boullion cubes
2 links sweet sausage
½ cup spaghetti sauce
½ cup pineapple juice
½ cup chopped ham
¼ cup slivered almonds
4 teaspoons butter or margarine
2 chicken boullion cubes
1 teaspoon curry powder
1 apple
2 green onions
2 small eggs
2 teaspoons soy sauce

Sausage and Pepper Hero

Objective: Make a sandwich big enough for a crowd.

Notes: This basic sausage and pepper recipe can be served in a variety of ways. This recipe suggests making a sandwich. It could also be served over rice or with noodles. If preferred, 12 individual sandwich rolls could be substituted for the Italian bread.

Shopping list for 12 students (working as 1 group):

    two 15-inch loaves Italian bread
    2 pounds sweet Italian sausage lengths
    3 large green peppers
    2 large onions
    1 can (29-ounces) crushed tomatoes
    1 teaspoon salt
    ½ teaspoon dried basil
    ½ teaspoon dried oregano
    ¼ teaspoon black pepper
    8 ounces mozzarella cheese

Scones & Strawberry Jam

Objectives:
1. Prepare English scones.
2. Make a quick jam.

Notes: Scones are a traditional English bread. If students have made biscuits, they will quickly see that scones include the same ingredients. The only difference is the shape in which they are made.

Shopping list for 12 students (3 groups):

    3 cups flour (plus flour for rolling out dough)
    1½ tablespoons baking powder
    ¾ teaspoon salt
    1 cup sugar (perhaps a little more for sprinkling scones)
    6 tablespoons butter or margarine
    ¾ cup cream
    3 eggs
    one 10-ounce package frozen strawberries

Snow Ice Cream

Objective: Use snow for a sweet treat.

Notes: This recipe is a fun treat for a snowy day, or finely crushed ice could be substituted for the snow.

Shopping list for 12 students (working individually):

    8 cups milk
    1 dozen eggs
    1½ cups sugar
    6 tablespoons vanilla

Stuffed Pasta Shells

Objectives:
1. Use a new kind of pasta.
2. Prepare a cheese filling for pasta.

Notes: For ease in stuffing the shells, be sure they are not overcooked. If they have cooked too long, they will be soft and break easily.

Students will be attracted to preparing this "fancy" dish.

Shopping list for 12 students (3 groups):

    ¾ pound jumbo macaroni shells (about 24 shells)
    1½ pounds ricotta cheese
    6 ounces mozzarella cheese
    3 small eggs
    6 saltine crackers
    2¼ teaspoons dried parsley
    ¾ teaspoon salt
    black pepper (not more than ¼ teaspoon)
    6 tablespoons grated Parmesan cheese
    1½ pints meatless spaghetti sauce

Stuffed Pita Pockets

Objective: Make a sandwich in pocket bread.

Notes: This is only one of an infinite number of possible fillings for pita bread. Fillings can be hot or cold.

White or whole-wheat pitas are both available and either can be used in this recipe.

Shopping list for 12 students (3 groups):

    3 small onions
    6 tablespoons butter or margarine
    1½ pounds ground beef

       1½ teaspoons salt
       ¾ teaspoon black pepper
       3 tablespoons chopped dill
       3 medium tomatoes
       6 pieces of pita bread
       1 head of lettuce

Sweet & Sour Meatballs

Objectives: 1. Make meatballs.
                  2. Try a new recipe for hamburg.

Notes: All students will be able to help shape the meatballs.

Shopping list for 12 students (3 groups):

       3 slices soft bread
       2¼ pounds ground beef
       1½ teaspoons salt
       3 eggs
       3 tablespoons oil
       9 carrots
       9 stalks celery
       3 green peppers
       6 tablespoons soy sauce
       3 tablespoons cider vinegar
       ¾ teaspoon ground ginger
       three 8-ounce cans pineapple chunks
       3 tablespoons cornstarch

Tomato Flower

Objectives: 1. Make egg salad.
                  2. Use a blender.

Notes: If preferred, the eggs can be cooked ahead for students to use in their salads.

Shopping list for 12 students (working individually):

       1 dozen eggs
       12 large tomatoes
       6 stalks celery
       ¾ cup mayonnaise
       2 tablespoons minced onion
       paprika (not more than 2 teaspoons)

Tomato Soup

Objectives: 1. Make soup from tomatoes.
2. Use a blender.

Notes: Nearly everyone has had tomato soup from a can, but it is difficult to associate that soup with an actual tomato. This recipe will help students make the connection.

Be sure students are careful using the blender. Starting it at too high a setting could result in hot tomatoes being sprayed around the room.

Shopping list for 12 students (working individually):

12 large ripe tomatoes
¼ cup butter or margarine
2 tablespoons granulated chicken boullion
3 cups milk or cream
salt (not more than 1 teaspoon)
black pepper (not more than ½ teaspoon)
celery leaves from one bunch of celery

Tossed Salad

Objectives: 1. Prepare vegetables for a salad.
2. Make a salad dressing.

Notes: This large-group recipe provides an activity for each of 12 students. Eleven students can each prepare a vegetable while the twelfth student prepares the dressing.

Other vegetables can be substituted according to what is available.

Shopping list for 12 students (working as 1 group):

1 head lettuce
2 large tomatoes
1 large purple onion
2 carrots
1 green pepper
½ pound fresh mushrooms
3 stalks celery
1 small cucumber
1 stalk broccoli

½ small head of cauliflower
6 to 8 radishes
1 can condensed tomato soup
¼ cup sugar
⅓ cup salad oil
⅓ cup cider vinegar
1 teaspoon garlic powder
1 teaspoon celery salt

Tuna Cheesie

Objectives: 1. Make a variation of the traditional tuna sandwich.

Notes: Students can put their sandwiches together on one or two broiler pans for cooking. There is no need to have a separate pan for each student.

Take the opportunity to talk with students about different ways tuna is packed. Some is packed in oil and other tuna is packed in water.

Shopping list for 12 students (working individually):

    2 cans (6½ ounces) tuna
    3 small onions
    3 sticks celery
    ¼ cup mayonnaise
    salt (not more than ½ teaspoon)
    ½ dozen English muffins
    2 medium-sized tomatoes
    12 slices American cheese

Vegetable Bouquet

Objectives: 1. Prepare raw vegetables for serving.
              2. Arrange vegetables for an attractive buffet setting.

Notes: A number of different holders can be used for the base of this bouquet. Other fruits to hold the toothpicks might be an apple or a grapefruit. An eggplant would also work. For something quite different, a piece of styrofoam in the shape of a cone could be used. Weight the bottom and add vegetables on toothpicks to decorate the tree.

Shopping list for 12 students (working individually):

    12 celery stalks
    12 carrots
    3 to 4 dozen radishes
    3 to 4 dozen cherry tomatoes
    ¾ cup whipped cream cheese
    12 oranges
    toothpicks

Vegetable Sampler (3 Recipes)

Objectives: 1. Prepare a variety of vegetables.
2. Sample several different ways of cooking vegetables.

Notes: For these recipes, fresh vegetables have been used. If it is easier, they can be adapted for use with frozen vegetables. Change cooking times in accordance with package directions.

Shopping list for 12 students (3 groups, each making a different recipe):

1 pound fresh green beans
1 pound carrots
3 ears fresh corn
1½ teaspoons salt
9 tablespoons butter
¼ cup sliced almonds
1 orange
⅔ cup orange juice
2 tablespoons brown sugar
⅛ teaspoon ground nutmeg
1 clove garlic
¼ green pepper
2 tablespoons sesame seeds
¼ teaspoon basil
⅛ teaspoon black pepper

Waldorf Salad

Objective: Combine fruit and vegetables in this salad.

Notes: There are several variations on the Waldorf salad. Some add nuts; some add raisins. By preparing individual salads, students can choose which ingredients they will include and which they would prefer to omit.

Shopping list for 12 students (working individually):

12 medium, bright red eating apples
12 stalks celery
1½ cups walnuts
1½ cups raisins
1½ to 2 cups mayonnaise or salad dressing

Walnut Chicken & Rice

Objectives: 1. Prepare a main-dish recipe.
2. Combine a variety of food textures in one dish.

Notes: A wok can be used for this recipe, but is not essential. A large saucepan will work quite well.

Shopping list for 12 students (3 groups):

    3 boneless chicken breasts
    1½ teaspoons ground ginger
    ¾ cup salad oil
    6 tablespoons soy sauce
    3 tablespoons cornstarch
    3 medium onions
    3 red bell peppers
    3 stalks broccoli
    3 chicken boullion cubes
    1½ cups walnuts
    2 cups rice
    1½ teaspoons salt

Welsh Rarebit

Objectives: 1. Prepare a cheesy lunch.
2. Learn to make a white sauce.

Notes: Who doesn't remember thinking this was a rabbit dish? It never quite made sense where the rabbit was in the final dish, but it sure sounded like that in the name!

Saltine crackers can be substituted for the toast. Serve the cheese sauce over 4 or 5 crackers.

Shopping list for 12 students (working individually):

    ¾ cup butter or margarine
    ¾ cup flour
    dry mustard (not more than 1½ teaspoons)
    salt (not more than 1 teaspoon)
    pepper (not more than 1 teaspoon)
    Worcestershire sauce (not more than 1 tablespoon)
    4 cups milk
    1½ pounds (approximately) cheddar cheese
    12 slices bread
    paprika (not more than 1½ teaspoons)

How to Play NUTRO

Teacher Instructions:

You will need to distribute a copy of the NUTRO worksheet with directions and playing card to each student. Students should prepare paper or cardboard strips to cover blocks on the cards as they are called.

You should also prepare the cards for the caller in advance. You will need nine index cards—four white and five of another color. Print the name of one of the four basic food groups on each white card: fruit and vegetables; dairy; bread and cereals; and meat and protein. On the colored cards print one of each of the letters in N-U-T-R-O.

Caller Instructions:

To play, the caller shuffles the nine index cards, draws one white and one colored card, and announces what they are: for instance, "T—dairy." All the players look in their "T" column to see if they have listed any dairy foods there. If so, they can cover it. Only one square can be covered with each call.

Play continues in this manner until a player covers five squares in a row horizontally, vertically, or diagonally.

NUTRO
The game with food for thought

Think of foods in the 4 basic food groups: 1) fruits and vegetables, 2) dairy products, 3) meat and protein, 4) bread and cereals. Try to think of 4 or 5 foods in each group until you have 24 in all. Write the names of the foods in the empty squares below.

NUTRO is played simlar to bingo. For each play, the caller will call one of the letters in the word NUTRO, then the name of a food group. For example, he or she will call "T—Dairy." If you have written the name of the dairy product in the T-column of your card, cover the square in which it is written. You may cover only one square at a time.

The first player to cover five squares in a row—vertical, horizontal, or diagonal—WINS THE GAME!

N	U	T	R	O
		FREE SQUARE MEAL		

© 1987 J. Weston Walch, Publisher   *62 Easy and Delicious Cooking Activities*

NAME _____ DATE _____

Amazing soup (SERVINGS: 12)

A recipe for soup that's different every time!

Ingredients:

    1 pound ground beef
    one 10-ounce can condensed
        cream of celery soup
    2 teaspoons dried parsley
    12 small cans (4 to 6 ounces)
        of a variety of vegetables: peas,
        corn, carrots, mushrooms, beans,
        etc.

Utensils:

Dutch oven or large soup kettle
wooden spoon
slotted spoon
paper towels
can or container for grease
can opener
measuring spoons
12 small soup bowls
12 soupspoons

Directions:

_____ 1. Break up the ground beef and put it in the Dutch oven.

_____ 2. Cook over medium heat. Stir the ground beef with a wooden spoon. Cook until there is no pink color left in the meat (about 10 minutes).

_____ 3. With a slotted spoon, remove cooked meat from the pan. Put it on a paper towel to drain.

_____ 4. Pour the remaining grease out of the pan.

_____ 5. Return the meat to the kettle.

_____ 6. Stir in can of soup.

_____ 7. Mix in parsley. Return mixture to heat.

_____ 8. Open cans of vegetables. Do not drain. One at a time, add cans of vegetables with liquid to the soup. Heat to serving temperature, stirring occasionally.

Bonus Activity: Making soup is a great way to use leftovers. Check the refrigerator at home. What leftovers are there that could be used in soup? Are there vegetables? Is there meat that could be used instead of chopped beef? Write a recipe for soup using what is available.

© 1987 J. Weston Walch, Publisher   62 Easy and Delicious Cooking Activities

NAME _____ DATE _____

Ambrosia (SERVINGS: 4)

This old favorite is especially popular in the South.

Ingredients:

    2 large Valencia oranges
    2 ripe bananas
    ½ pineapple
    1 cup shredded coconut
    ¼ cup confectioners' sugar

Utensils:

    paring knife
    chopping board
    small bowl
    spoon for mixing
    4 glass dessert dishes
    4 spoons

Directions:

_____ 1. Peel the oranges, removing all membrane. Break into sections and cut each section in half.

_____ 2. Peel the bananas. Cut in thin slices.

_____ 3. Remove peel from pineapple. Cut away core. Cut fruit into bite-size pieces.

_____ 4. Combine coconut and confectioners' sugar in small bowl. Mix together.

_____ 5. In each serving dish, put a layer of orange pieces. Then put a layer of bananas, followed by a layer of pineapple. Sprinkle with a layer of coconut mixture. Continue alternating layers, ending with coconut topping. Serve chilled.

Bonus Activity: Try using a fresh coconut for this recipe. In addition to the coconut, you'll need a glass, a paring knife, a grater, a hammer, and a nail.

    There is milk in a fresh coconut. Use the hammer and nail to make a hole in the coconut. Pour the milk into the glass.

    With a hammer, break the coconut into 3 or 4 pieces. Use a paring knife to remove the white meat from the shell. Grate it into fine pieces.

© 1987 J. Weston Walch, Publisher   *62 Easy and Delicious Cooking Activities*

NAME _____ DATE _____

Apple Turnover (SERVINGS: 1)

This pastry is not as difficult as you might think!

Ingredients:

¼ cup flour
pinch of salt
1 tablespoon vegetable
 shortening
1½ teaspoons cold water
½ apple
1 tablespoon granulated sugar
¼ teaspoon cinnamon
flour for rolling out dough
confectioners' sugar to dust
 turnover

Utensils:

2 small mixing bowls
fork
rolling pin
paring knife
chopping board
spoon for mixing
baking sheet
wire cooling rack
spatula

Directions:

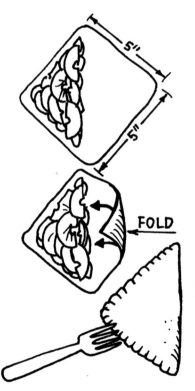

1. Preheat oven to 425°.
2. Measure flour and salt into one bowl.
3. Add shortening. Use fingers to blend shortening and dry ingredients together.
4. Add cold water and mix with fork to form dough. It may be necessary to add a drop or two more water.
5. Peel apple half. Remove core. Slice apple into bowl.
6. Add sugar and cinnamon to apple. Mix well.
7. On floured surface, roll dough into 5" x 5" square.
8. Place filling on half of square as shown.
9. Wet the edges of the square. Fold dough to enclose filling in a triangle. Seal edges by pressing with a fork.
10. Put turnover on baking sheet and bake 15 minutes until lightly browned.
11. Remove to cooling rack. Sprinkle with confectioners' sugar if desired.

(Continued on next sheet.)

NAME _____ DATE _____

Apple Turnover (continued)

Bonus Activity: Compare the cost of making your own turnovers with turnovers you might purchase at the bakery or supermarket. How much did it cost for each ingredient? What was the total cost? (It might be easier to estimate the costs for making a dozen turnovers.)

Check your costs with the prices at bakeries and supermarkets. How do they compare? How do the flavors compare? How much time is required from you to serve each different kind?

NAME _____ DATE _____

Beef Stroganoff (SERVINGS: 4)

This dish is named after Count Paul Stroganoff, a 19th-century Russian diplomat.

Ingredients:

    one 8-ounce package fine egg noodles
    water for cooking noodles
    1-pound beef tenderloin
    1 medium onion
    ¼-pound fresh mushrooms
    2 tablespoons butter or margarine (divided)
    1 teaspoon dry mustard
    dash of black pepper
    one 10½-ounce can condensed cream of mushroom soup
    ½ cup sour cream
    ¼ cup water

Utensils:

    saucepan with cover
    wooden spoon
    knife
    chopping board
    10-inch skillet
    can opener
    colander

    4 luncheon plates
    4 forks

Directions:

_____ 1. Half fill saucepan with water. Cover. Bring to a boil.

_____ 2. Add noodles to water. Stir until water returns to boil.

_____ 3. Cover. Turn off heat. Let cook 15 minutes.

(Continued on next sheet.)

NAME _____ DATE _____

Beef Stroganoff (continued)

_____ 4. Trim fat from steak. Cut meat across grain in ½-inch slices. Cut each slice into 2-inch strips.

_____ 5. Dry strips on paper towels.

_____ 6. Peel onion and chop.

_____ 7. Slice mushrooms.

_____ 8. Melt 1 tablespoon butter in skillet.

_____ 9. Cook meat in butter, stirring constantly until lightly browned.

_____ 10. Remove meat from pan.

_____ 11. Melt additional tablespoon of butter.

_____ 12. Add onion, mushrooms, mustard, and pepper to the pan. Cook, stirring frequently, until vegetables are tender.

_____ 13. Stir in undiluted soup.

_____ 14. Mix in sour cream.

_____ 15. Stir in water.

_____ 16. Add meat and heat through.

_____ 17. Drain noodles in colander. Put on plates.

_____ 18. Serve beef sauce over hot noodles.

Bonus Activity: This recipe was named after a Russian diplomat. We therefore assume that it included some of his favorite foods and flavors.

What food would you like to have named after you? What are your favorite flavor combinations? Write out a recipe that you would like to have historians name for you.

© 1987 J. Weston Walch, Publisher   *62 Easy and Delicious Cooking Activities*

NAME _____ DATE _____

Beverages (SERVINGS: 1)

A rainbow of refreshing thirst quenchers!

Banana Shake

1 small ripe banana
½ cup milk
½ teaspoon almond flavoring
sprinkle of grated nutmeg

measuring cup
measuring spoon
blender
glass

1. Peel banana. Break into 3 or 4 pieces. Put in blender.
2. Add milk and flavoring.
3. Blend until smooth.
4. Pour into tall glass.
5. Sprinkle with nutmeg.

Fruit Juice Bubbly

1 large juice orange
½ cup ginger ale or club soda
crushed ice

orange juicer
measuring cup
tall glass
spoon

1. Use juicer to extract juice from orange.
2. Put in glass.
3. Add ginger ale or club soda.
4. Pour juice into glass. Mix well.

Eggnog

1 small egg
1 cup milk
1 teaspoon vanilla extract
sprinkle of nutmeg

small bowl
measuring cup
measuring spoon
whisk or eggbeater
glass

1. Break egg into bowl. Beat with whisk or eggbeater for about 1 minute.
2. Add milk.
3. Add flavoring. Beat mixture again.
4. Pour into glass. Sprinkle with nutmeg.

(Continued on next sheet.)

© 1987 J. Weston Walch, Publisher   *62 Easy and Delicious Cooking Activities*

Beverages (continued)

Fruit Shake

¼ cantaloupe
½ cup apple juice
crushed ice

paring knife
chopping board
measuring cup
blender
tall glass

1. Remove seeds from cantaloupe. Cut off peel. Cut fruit into 1-inch cubes.
2. Place juice and fruit in blender. Starting with slowest speed, blend until smooth.
3. Pour in glass of crushed ice.

Bonus Activity: What favorite flavors would you like to combine in a drink? Which flavors do you prefer? Write a recipe for your own thirst quencher!

© 1987 J. Weston Walch, Publisher   *62 Easy and Delicious Cooking Activities*

NAME _____ DATE _____

Breakfast Pizza (SERVINGS: 1)

Do you like pizza? Try this variation for breakfast.

Ingredients:

    ½ English muffin
    1 slice bacon
    1 egg
    2 tablespoons pizza sauce
    1 teaspoon grated Parmesan cheese

Utensils:

    toaster
    small skillet
    paper towel
    can or container for grease
    spatula
    wooden spoon
    luncheon plate
    fork

Directions:

1. Toast the English muffin. Place on a plate.
2. In a skillet, fry the bacon until crisp. Drain on a paper towel.
3. Reduce the heat. Break the egg into the skillet and cook to desired firmness.
4. Slide egg onto the muffin.
5. Crumble the crisp bacon over the egg.
6. Pour excess fat out of the skillet.
7. Heat pizza sauce and pour over egg.
8. Sprinkle cheese over all.

Bonus Activity: Pizza has almost as many variations as there are people who make it. Make a list of pizza variations. Just one rule to this game—each variation on the list has to be something that is actually served in a public restaurant or store.

    Who in your class has the longest list of variations? Who has the strangest variation? Which pizza do you prefer? Which do you think is the most popular?

© 1987 J. Weston Walch, Publisher   62 *Easy and Delicious Cooking Activities*

Butter-Crumb Vegetables (SERVINGS: 4)

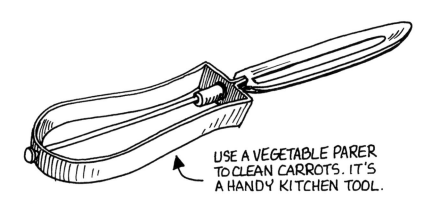

USE A VEGETABLE PARER TO CLEAN CARROTS. IT'S A HANDY KITCHEN TOOL.

A variety of vegetables is used to make this a colorful dish!

Ingredients:

    1 small cauliflower
    ¼ head red cabbage
    3 medium carrots
    1½ cups bok choy greens
    water for cooking vegetables
    2 tablespoons butter
    1 clove garlic
    4 slices whole grain bread
    fresh black pepper

Utensils:

    paring knife
    chopping board
    cabbage shredder
    vegetable parer
    vegetable steamer
    garlic press
    heavy skillet
    wooden spoon
    1½-quart casserole dish
    4 luncheon plates
    4 forks

Directions:

_____ 1. Preheat oven to 500°.

_____ 2. Break cauliflower into small flowerets.

_____ 3. Shred cabbage with shredder.

(Continued on next sheet.)

NAME _____ DATE _____

Butter-Crumb Vegetables (continued)

_____   4. Pare carrots. Cut into ½-inch slices.

_____   5. Wash bok choy and cut into small pieces.

_____   6. Bring water in vegetable steamer to a boil.

_____   7. Place cauliflower, cabbage, and carrots in steamer. Cover and cook 8 to 9 minutes or until just barely tender.

_____   8. Add bok choy and steam 1 minute more to wilt greens.

_____   9. Cut bread into tiny pieces.

_____   10. Melt 2 tablespoons butter in skillet.

_____   11. Mince garlic and sauté in butter.

_____   12. Toss bread crumbs in garlic butter until butter is absorbed and crumbs are evenly coated.

_____   13. Put steamed vegetables in casserole dish.

_____   14. Sprinkle with black pepper.

_____   15. Add half of crumb topping and mix well.

_____   16. Spread vegetables in casserole dish.

_____   17. Top with remaining crumbs.

_____   18. Bake in oven for 5 minutes.

_____   19. Serve hot.

Bonus Activity: Color can be one consideration in choosing a vegetable to serve. It is important to consider how food will look on a plate. If you are serving white fish, you might not want to also serve white potatoes and white parsnips on the same plate!

Classify vegetables according to color. Under the word "green," write all the green vegetables you know. What other colors can vegetables be? Write a list of vegetables for each color.

© 1987 J. Weston Walch, Publisher   62 Easy and Delicious Cooking Activities

NAME _____ DATE _____

Butterscotch Biscuits (SERVINGS: 4)

If biscuits are this easy to make, who needs a mix?

Ingredients: **Utensils:**

½ cup flour   small mixing bowl
1¼ teaspoons baking powder   measuring spoons
¼ teaspoon sugar   wooden spoon
1 tablespoon margarine or butter   rolling pin
¼ cup milk   small saucepan
flour for rolling out dough   baking sheet
2 tablespoons brown sugar   cooling rack
1½ teaspoons melted margarine or butter   spatula

Directions:

_____   1. Preheat oven to 425°.
_____   2. Measure flour, baking powder, and sugar into the bowl.
_____   3. Add butter. With fingers, mix butter and dry ingredients together.
_____   4. Add milk. Stir until just mixed.
_____   5. Toss a few times on floured surface.
_____   6. Roll into a rectangle about ¼ inch thick.
_____   7. Melt butter in small pan. Spread over dough.
_____   8. Sprinkle with brown sugar.
_____   9. Roll up jelly-roll fashion, pinching seam to seal.
_____ 10. Cut into 4 pieces. Place on baking sheet.
_____ 11. Bake for 10 minutes or until lightly browned.
_____ 12. Place a wire rack to cool.

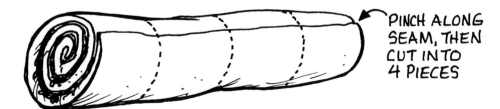

PINCH ALONG SEAM, THEN CUT INTO 4 PIECES

Bonus Activity: To make 12 biscuits instead of 4, how much of each ingredient will you need?

© 1987 J. Weston Walch Publisher   *62 Easy and Delicious Cooking Activities*

NAME _____ DATE _____

Carrot-Potato Cake (SERVINGS: 1)

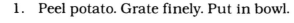

It's not french fries or hash browns; it's better!

Ingredients: **Utensils:**

  1 medium potato   paring knife
  1 medium carrot   vegetable parer
  ¼ small onion   vegetable grater
  1 tablespoon butter or margarine   chopping board
  sprinkle of salt   mixing bowl
                               fork for mixing
                               small skillet
                               spatula
                               paper towel

Directions:

1. Peel potato. Grate finely. Put in bowl.
2. Peel carrot. Grate finely. Add to bowl.
3. Peel onion. Chop very fine. Add to bowl.
4. Add salt. Use fork to mix all ingredients well.
5. Heat skillet over medium heat. Melt butter.
6. Put vegetable mixture in the pan. Use spatula to shape mixture into a flat round cake.
7. Cook until brown on one side. Flip over to brown on the second side.
8. Remove from pan and put on paper towel to drain extra grease.
9. Eat while still warm.

Bonus Activity: How might this recipe be served? What meal could you use it with? What other foods might be served to round out the meal? Select other foods or recipes to serve with carrot-potato cakes. Write out your menu.

© 1987 J. Weston Walch, Publisher   *62 Easy and Delicious Cooking Activities*

NAME _____ DATE _____

Cheddar Cheese Crackers (SERVINGS: 1)

These cheesy crackers are delicious with peanut butter!

Ingredients:

¼ cup flour
¼ teaspoon salt
sprinkle of ground ginger
sprinkle of granulated sugar
¼ cup cheddar cheese (about 1 ounce)
1 tablespoon butter or margarine
1 teaspoon egg yolk
1 teaspoon cold water
1 tablespoon toasted sesame seeds
flour for rolling out dough

Utensils:

small mixing bowl
measuring spoons
measuring cup
cheese grater
fork for mixing
rolling pin
baking sheet
knife
spatula
wire cooling rack

Directions:

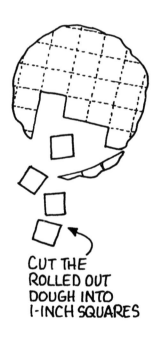

CUT THE ROLLED OUT DOUGH INTO 1-INCH SQUARES

1. Preheat oven to 350°.
2. Combine flour, salt, ginger, and sugar in a bowl.
3. Grate cheese to make ¼ cup. Add to dry ingredients.
4. Put butter in bowl. Use fingers to mix butter with dry ingredients until mixture resembles coarse crumbs.
5. With fork, stir in egg yolk, cold water, and sesame seeds.
6. Mix well and shape into a ball. If necessary, add additional water a drop at a time.
7. With floured rolling pin on a floured surface, roll out dough to ⅛-inch thickness.
8. Cut into 1-inch square cracker shapes.
9. Lift with spatula to ungreased baking sheet.
10. Bake 12 to 15 minutes until crackers are lightly browned.
11. Cool on wire rack.

Bonus Activity: Find recipes for yeast bread, muffins, and biscuits. Compare these three recipes with this recipe for crackers. How are they similar? How are they different?

What ingredients are in all four foods? What leavening is used in each? How much sweetener is included in each of the recipes? What provides the major flavor?

© 1987 J. Weston Walch, Publisher   *62 Easy and Delicious Cooking Activities*

NAME _____ DATE _____

Cheese Dog (SERVINGS: 1)

A new wrapping on the traditional hot dog.

Ingredients:

1 hot dog
1 slice American cheese
1 slice bacon
1 hot dog bun

Utensils:

paring knife
2 toothpicks
broiler pan

Directions:

1. Preheat oven to broil.
2. Make a lengthwise slice in the hot dog, not cutting through completely.
3. Cut the cheese into ½-inch wide strips.
4. Place the strips in the hot dog.
5. Wrap a strip of bacon around each hot dog. Slant the bacon so that it will extend from one end to the other. Fasten the ends of the bacon to the hot dog with toothpicks.
6. Place on broiler pan and broil 5 inches from the heat about 10 minutes. Turn when bacon is crisp.
7. Serve in hot dog bun.

SLIT THE HOT DOG AND PUT CHEESE STRIPS IN SLIT

THEN WRAP THE DOG AND CHEESE IN A STRIP OF BACON

Bonus Activity: Do you call this a meat a hot dog or a frankfurter or do you have another name for it? Are there some distinctions in your mind between frankfurters and hot dogs?

What can you learn about the history of this food? Where were the first ones made? Who originated them? How did they become popular? What are they made from today?

© 1987 J. Weston Walch, Publisher   *62 Easy and Delicious Cooking Activities*

NAME _____ DATE _____

Cheese Soup (SERVINGS: 1)

This soup will warm your insides on the coldest winter day.

Ingredients:

½ small onion
⅓ cup shredded Swiss cheese (about 1½ ounces)
½ slice pumpernickel bread
1 tablespoon butter or margarine
1 tablespoon flour
1 cup milk
1 teaspoon chopped parsley

Utensils:

paring knife
chopping board
cheese grater
measuring cup
measuring spoons
small saucepan
toaster
wooden spoon

soup bowl
soupspoon

Directions:

1. Peel onion and chop finely.
2. Grate cheese.
3. Toast bread and cut into small cubes.
4. Melt butter in saucepan.
5. Cook onions until tender, about 5 minutes. Stir to prevent the onions from scorching.
6. Add flour and mix well.
7. Add ¼ of the milk and stir until thickened.
8. Add remaining milk and heat to simmering, stirring all the time.
9. Add parsley.
10. Remove from heat. Stir in cheese.
11. When cheese has melted, pour into bowl and garnish with pumpernickel cubes.

Bonus Activity: Swiss cheese is used in this recipe, but it could have been cheddar or some other kind of cheese.

What kinds of cheese are available at the store where you shop? Are there additional kinds available at a cheese specialty store? What other kinds of cheese could have been substituted in this recipe?

© 1987 J. Weston Walch, Publisher   *62 Easy and Delicious Cooking Activities*

Chicken Noodle Soup (SERVINGS: 4)

Cellophane noodles are available in oriental food stores.

Ingredients:

  2 cups water
  ½ chicken breast
  1 bunch cellophane noodles
     (about 1 ounce)
  2 scallions
  2 teaspoons soy sauce
  pepper

Utensils:

  medium-sized saucepan and cover
  small bowl
  paring knife
  chopping board
  measuring cup
  measuring spoons
  wooden spoon
  kitchen scissors

  4 small serving bowls
  4 soupspoons

Directions:

_____ 1. Place the chicken in the saucepan with water. Bring the water to a boil and cook for 3 minutes.

_____ 2. Lower the heat. Cover and simmer for 20 minutes.

_____ 3. Put the cellophane noodles in a small bowl and cover with warm water. Let soak 10 minutes.

(Continued on next sheet.)

© 1987 J. Weston Walch, Publisher

62 Easy and Delicious Cooking Activities

NAME _____ DATE _____

Chicken Noodle Soup (continued)

_____ 4. Finely chop the scallions, both green and white parts.

_____ 5. When the chicken is cooked, remove it from the broth.

_____ 6. When chicken is cool enough to handle, remove the skin and bone. Use a knife to cut the meat into thin strips.

_____ 7. Bring the chicken broth to a boil.

_____ 8. Stir the soy sauce into the broth.

_____ 9. Season with pepper.

_____ 10. Add the chicken strips and chopped scallions. Cook for 1 minute.

_____ 11. Use kitchen scissors to cut noodles. Put ¼ of noodles into each bowl.

_____ 12. Pour the soup over the noodles. Serve hot.

Bonus Activity: Chicken noodle soup has become known as a remedy if you are not feeling well. People fix chicken noodle soup to serve someone confined to bed with a cold.

Other foods have strong associations for people too. We have turkey at Thanksgiving or watermelon on the fourth of July. In addition, many families have their own personal food associations. There is a special recipe for birthdays or one certain dish that is Sunday-night supper.

What food associations come to your mind? Write as many as you can think of. Share them with your classmates.

© 1987 J. Weston Walch, Publisher   *62 Easy and Delicious Cooking Activities*

NAME _____ DATE _____

Chili (SERVINGS: 4)

This favorite main dish comes from "south of the border."

Ingredients:

    1 small onion
    1 medium clove garlic
    1 tablespoon butter or margarine
    ½ pound ground beef
    ½ green pepper
    1 teaspoon chili powder
    ¼ teaspoon basil
    1 cup tomatoes with juice
    1 cup kidney beans with liquid

Utensils:

    paring knife
    chopping board
    garlic press
    medium-sized skillet
    measuring spoons
    wooden spoon
    4 small serving dishes
    4 spoons

Directions:

_____ 1. Peel and chop onion.

_____ 2. Peel garlic clove and put through press.

_____ 3. Melt the butter in the skillet, over low heat.

_____ 4. Add onion and garlic. Sauté until soft and golden. Stir occasionally.

_____ 5. Add the beef and stir until browned.

_____ 6. Remove seeds from the green pepper. Dice.

_____ 7. Add green pepper to the meat mixture.

_____ 8. Add chili powder and basil.

_____ 9. Measure tomatoes. Be sure tomatoes are chopped. Add to the meat mixture.

_____ 10. Add beans. Let mixture simmer 15 minutes until ready to serve.

_____ 11. Pour chili into serving dishes.

Bonus Activity: Find recipes for chili in several cookbooks. How do they compare?

    What ingredients are always included in chili—indeed, have to be included for it to be called chili? Is each food always in the same proportion? For example, how much chili powder per serving is called for in each recipe?

    Which recipe looks the easiest to prepare? Which recipe takes the longest time? Do any of the recipes have special taste secrets?

© 1987 J. Weston Walch, Publisher   *62 Easy and Delicious Cooking Activities*

NAME _____ DATE _____

Chow Mein (SERVINGS: 12)

Use Chinese noodles for chow mein or serve with rice for chop suey!

Ingredients:

    1 pound pork steak
    1 large onion
    6 stalks celery
    ½ large green pepper
    ¼ pound mushrooms
    8-ounce can water chestnuts
    1-pound can bean sprouts
    3 tablespoons cooking oil
    1½ tablespoons cornstarch
    1½ tablespoons soy sauce
    2 tablespoons water
    1 cup water
    5-ounce can Chinese noodles

Utensils:

    paring knife
    chopping board
    can opener
    small bowl
    measuring spoons
    measuring cup
    large frying pan or Dutch oven
    wooden spoon
    slotted spoon
    paper towel
    oven-proof bowl (Pyrex)
    12 luncheon plates
    12 forks

Directions:

_____ 1. Trim fat from pork steak. Cut the pork steak into thin strips.

_____ 2. Peel the onion. Cut in half and slice both halves.

_____ 3. Wash celery and slice.

_____ 4. Remove seeds from pepper and chop.

_____ 5. Cut mushrooms into thin slices.

_____ 6. Drain water chestnuts. Slice thinly.

_____ 7. Drain bean sprouts. Rinse with cold water to crisp sprouts.

_____ 8. Measure soy sauce, cornstarch, and 2 tablespoons water. Mix together in small bowl.

_____ 9. Put Chinese noodles in oven-proof bowl. Place in 300° oven to heat for 10 minutes.

_____ 10. Heat oil in frying pan.

_____ 11. Add pork and brown in the oil. Use slotted spoon to remove pork to paper towel to drain.

_____ 12. Cook the onions, green pepper, and celery in the frying pan.

_____ 13. When they begin to soften, add mushrooms and water chestnuts.

(Continued on next sheet.)

NAME _____ DATE _____

Chow Mein (continued)

_____ 14. Add 1 cup water and let cook 2 to 3 minutes.

_____ 15. Add soy sauce-cornstarch mixture. Stir until thickened.

_____ 16. Mix in bean sprouts and pork. Warm through.

_____ 17. Put noodles on each plate. Top with vegetable-pork mixture.

Bonus Activity: Canned chow mein can be purchased in the grocery store. Look at a label to determine what ingredients are in the canned product. The order in which ingredients are listed is important. The can contains the largest amount of the first item, second largest amount of the first item, second largest amount of the second item, and so forth.

If you were to can your chow mein, what information would you include on the label? What graphics would you include? Design a label for your chow mein.

© 1987 J. Weston Walch Publisher   *62 Easy and Delicious Cooking Activities*

NAME _____ DATE _____

Corn Chowder (SERVINGS: 4)

This chowder is hearty and filling enough to be a main course.

Ingredients:

- 4 slices bacon
- 1 small onion
- 2 medium potatoes
- 1 cup cream-style corn
- dash of pepper
- 2 cups of boiling water
- ½ cup half-and-half

Utensils:

- small frying pan
- paring knife
- chopping board
- medium-sized saucepan
- measuring spoon
- measuring cup
- wooden spoon
- paper towel
- soup ladle
- 4 soup bowls
- 4 soupspoons

Directions:

_____ 1. In a frying pan, cook the bacon until crisp. Remove to paper towel to drain.

_____ 2. Measure 2 tablespoons bacon fat into the saucepan.

_____ 3. Peel onion. Cut in half and cut into slices.

_____ 4. Cook onion in saucepan over low heat. Stir and do not let onion brown.

_____ 5. Peel the potatoes. Dice.

_____ 6. Add potatoes to the saucepan.

_____ 7. Add water and cook until the potatoes are tender—about 15 minutes.

_____ 8. Add pepper to taste.

_____ 9. Blend in corn and half-and-half. Let chowder heat through.

_____ 10. Ladle into 4 bowls.

_____ 11. Crumble bacon and sprinkle over each bowl of chowder.

Bonus Activity: What seasonings are included in this recipe? This is quite a basic recipe, but perhaps other herbs or spices could be added for a more distinctive flavoring.

Consult an herb chart. Many cookbooks include this kind of information. According to the chart, what herbs might be appropriate to add to soup or chowder or a corn dish? Which ones might you like to try in your chowder?

© 1987 J. Weston Walch, Publisher   *62 Easy and Delicious Cooking Activities*

Crepes (SERVINGS: 4)

ROTATE THE PAN UNTIL THE BATTER COVERS THE BOTTOM.

This relative of the pancake originated in France.

Ingredients:

¾ cup flour
1½ teaspoons sugar
¼ teaspoon baking powder
¼ teaspoon salt
1 cup milk
1 egg
¼ teaspoon vanilla
1 tablespoon margarine for pan
½ cup (approximately) strawberry jam
confectioners' sugar to sprinkle on
   crepes

Utensils:

medium-sized mixing bowl
small bowl
rotary beater
measuring spoons
measuring cup
spoon for mixing
10-inch skillet
spatula
knife

4 small dessert plates
4 forks

Directions:

_____ 1. Combine flour, sugar, baking powder, and salt in larger bowl.

_____ 2. In a separate bowl, mix together milk, eggs, and vanilla.

(Continued on next sheet.)

© 1987 J. Weston Walch, Publisher   62 Easy and Delicious Cooking Activities

NAME _____ DATE _____

Crepes (continued)

_____ 3. Pour liquid mixture into dry ingredients. Mix with spoon.

_____ 4. Beat with a rotary beater until smooth.

_____ 5. For each crepe, put small amount of butter in skillet. Heat over medium heat until butter is bubbly.

_____ 6. Pour about ¼ cup of batter into skillet and rotate pan until batter covers bottom.

_____ 7. Cook until the top seems dry and the bottom just begins to brown.

_____ 8. Slide spatula under crepe and turn with a quick flip. Brown the other side lightly.

_____ 9. Remove to plate. While still warm, spread with thin layer of jam.

_____ 10. Roll up. Sprinkle with confectioner's sugar.

Bonus Activity: Crepes do not have to be served only for dessert. What kind of filling could be used if you wanted to serve crepes as a main dish at lunch? Write out your recipe.

Confectioners' sugar probably would not be appropriate for the top. How would you garnish your crepes to give them eye-appeal?

© 1987 J. Weston Walch, Publisher   *62 Easy and Delicious Cooking Activities*

NAME _____ DATE _____

Dilly Dippers (SERVINGS: 4)

No need to wash the dish in which you serve this dip!

Ingredients:

    2 large carrots
    2 stalks of celery
    1 cucumber
    1/3 cup sour cream
    1 tablespoon mayonnaise
    1/2 teaspoon minced onion
    1/2 teaspoon dill weed
    1/2 teaspoon seasoned salt
    1 teaspoon dried parsley
    1 bulky roll

Utensils:

    vegetable parer
    paring knife
    cutting board
    fork
    small mixing bowl
    measuring cup
    measuring spoons
    spoon for mixing
    bread knife
    dinner plate

Directions:

_____ 1. Use a vegetable parer to scrape the skin off the carrots. Cut the ends off each carrot. Cut each carrot in half. Cut each piece lengthwise into 4 sticks.

_____ 2. Wash the celery. Use a paring knife to cut off the ends. Cut each stalk of celery lengthwise to make 2 pieces. Then cut the celery into pieces 3 inches long.

(Continued on next sheet.)

PRESS HARD ENOUGH WITH THE FORK TO BREAK THE CUCUMBER SKIN.

© 1987 J. Weston Walch, Publisher   62 Easy and Delicious Cooking Activities

NAME _____ DATE _____

Dilly Dippers (continued)

_____ 3. Wash the cucumber. Cut both ends off. Run a fork down the cucumber from end to end. Press hard enough to break the skin. Make this design all the way around the cucumber. Cut the cucumber into thin slices.

_____ 4. In a small bowl, mix together the sour cream, mayonnaise, minced onion, dill weed, seasoned salt, and parsley.

_____ 5. Use the roll to make a serving container for the dip. With the bread knife, cut a dish in the roll.

_____ 6. Place the roll in the middle of the plate. Spoon the dip into the hole in the roll. Arrange vegetables around the edge of the plate.

Bonus Activity: Imagine you are having a party where you will serve appetizers. Who will the guests be? How many people will be there? What kind of a party are you imagining?

Check several cookbooks to find recipes for appetizers that you might serve.

NAME _____   DATE _____

Egg Foo Yung (SERVINGS: 4)

A variety of fish or meat can be used in this recipe.

Ingredients:

- 4 eggs
- 2 green onions
- 1 tablespoon soy sauce
- 2 stalks celery
- ¼ green pepper
- 1 cup bean sprouts
- one 4½-ounce can tiny shrimp
  (or ½ cup cooked chicken or pork)
- 4 teaspoons cooking oil

Utensils:

- 2 small mixing bowls
- whisk
- paring knife
- cutting board
- measuring cup
- measuring spoons
- can opener
- fork for mixing
- small nonstick skillet
- spatula

- 4 luncheon plates
- 4 forks

Directions:

_____ 1. Break eggs into small bowl. Beat lightly with whisk.

_____ 2. Mix in soy sauce.

(Continued on next sheet.)

USE A SPATULA TO SHAPE THE MIXTURE INTO A CAKE

© 1987 J. Weston Walch, Publisher   62 Easy and Delicious Cooking Activities

NAME _____ DATE _____

Egg Foo Yung (continued)

_____ 3. Wash green onions and chop finely.

_____ 4. Wash celery stalks and chop finely.

_____ 5. Wash green pepper and chop finely.

_____ 6. Rinse bean sprouts with cold water.

_____ 7. Rinse shrimp with cold water.

_____ 8. Combine onions, celery, green pepper, bean sprouts, and shrimp in bowl. Mix with a fork.

_____ 9. Heat 1 teaspoon oil in frying pan.

_____ 10. Add ¼ of the sprout mixture.

_____ 11. Pour ¼ of egg over sprouts.

_____ 12. Use spatula to shape mixture into cake as it cooks.

_____ 13. When brown on one side, turn to brown on other.

_____ 14. Put on serving plate.

15. Repeat for 3 more servings.

Bonus Activity: Soy sauce is often included in Chinese cooking. What is soy sauce? Look at the label to see what it is made of.

How would you describe the flavor? What seasonings(s) are used as standards in American cooking the way soy sauce is used in Chinese cooking?

© 1987 J. Weston Walch, Publisher   62 Easy and Delicious Cooking Activities

Four-Square Tortilla (SERVINGS: 1)

There's something from every food group in this yummy sandwich!

Ingredients

- 1 tortilla
- 1 teaspoon mayonnaise
- 1 slice ham or salami
- ½ carrot
- ¼ cup alfalfa sprouts
- 1 slice cheese
- 1 lettuce leaf

Utensils:

- aluminum foil
- vegetable parer
- vegetable grater
- knife
- toothpick

Directions:

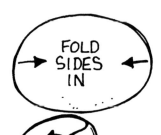

1. Preheat oven to 350°.
2. Wrap tortilla in aluminum foil.
3. Heat in oven for 15 minutes.
4. Peel carrot. Grate finely.
5. Spread heated tortilla with mayonnaise.
6. Lay lettuce leaf on mayonnaise.
7. Lay ham or salami slice over lettuce.
8. Put cheese over meat.
9. Spread grated carrot down center of tortilla.
10. Put sprouts over carrots.
11. Pull one side of tortilla over the center and then the other. Hold in place with a toothpick.

Bonus Activity: Nutrition experts report that it is essential to eat foods from each of four basic groups. Cut pictures from magazines to make a Basic-4 collage to show some of the foods that are in each of these four food groups.

   Divide the collage into 4 sections:
   1) fruit and vegetables,
   2) bread and cereals,
   3) dairy products, and
   4) meat and protein foods.

© 1987 J. Weston Walch, Publisher   62 *Easy and Delicious Cooking Activities*

NAME _____ DATE _____

Fruit Cones (SERVINGS: 12)

Here's a new filling for ice cream cones.

Ingredients:

12 ice cream cones (sugar)
1 cantaloupe
2 oranges
½ pound seedless grapes
2 bananas
2 apples
2 pears
2 peaches
1 pint strawberries
1 grapefruit
½ pineapple
¾ cup sour cream
2 tablespoons honey
2 tablespoons orange juice concentrate
½ cup walnuts

Utensils:

large bowl
2 spoons for mixing
paring knife
chopping board
small bowl
measuring cup
measuring spoon
nut chopper
colander

Directions:

_____ 1. Cantaloupe: cut fruit in quarters; remove seeds; peel; cut fruit in bite-sized pieces.

_____ 2. Oranges: peel fruit, removing as much white membrane as possible; break into sections; cut each section into 3 pieces; remove any seeds.

(Continued on next sheet.)

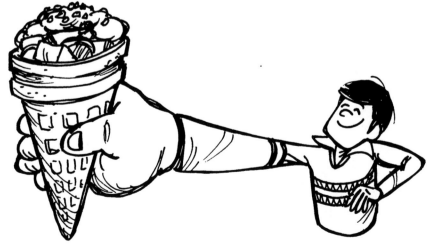

© 1987 J. Weston Walch, Publisher

62 Easy and Delicious Cooking Activities

NAME _____ DATE _____

Fruit Cones (continued)

_____ 3. Grapes: remove stems and any spoiled grapes; wash thoroughly.

_____ 4. Bananas: peel fruit; cut into bite-sized pieces.

_____ 5. Apples: wash fruit; cut into quarters; remove core; cut into bite-sized pieces.

_____ 6. Pears: wash fruit; cut into quarters; remove core; cut into bite-sized pieces.

_____ 7. Peaches: peel fruit; cut into half and remove pit; cut into bite-sized pieces.

_____ 8. Strawberries: remove hulls; wash and cut into bite-sized pieces.

_____ 9. Grapefruit: cut in half; cut around fruit in each half; use spoon to remove fruit sections from rind.

_____ 10. Pineapple: cut half into 2 quarters; remove peel and cut out core; cut fruit into bite-sized pieces.

_____ 11. Dressing: in small bowl, thoroughly mix sour cream, honey, and juice concentrate.

_____ 12. Chop nuts until very fine.

_____ 13. Combine fruit in large bowl.

_____ 14. Put in colander to drain juice.

_____ 15. When ready to serve, fill each cone with fruit.

_____ 16. Put spoonful of dressing on fruit.

_____ 17. Top each cone with chopped nuts.

Bonus Activity: Fruit salad is popular in the summer. It can be served as an appetizer, or dessert, or with cottage cheese for a light lunch.

An ice cream cone is one container that can be used for serving fruit. What other unusual serving "dishes" might be used for fruit salad? In what type of setting would each be appropriate? Cookbooks may be able to give you some ideas.

© 1987 J. Weston Walch, Publisher   62 Easy and Delicious Cooking Activities

NAME _____ DATE _____

Fruit Kabob (SERVINGS: 1)

Try this different way to serve a variety of fruits.

Ingredients

3 of the following fruits:

1/12 cantaloupe
4 or 5 strawberries
6 to 8 grapes
1/8 pound watermelon
1/2 peach
1/2 pear

Utensils:

paring knife
cutting board
1 wooden kabob stick

Directions:

1. In deciding which fruits to use, pick fruits that are in season. Choose fruits that offer a variety of colors and will look good together.

2. Prepare the fruit following the directions below:

    Cantaloupe: Scrape out the seeds. Cut off the skin. Cut fruit into 1-inch cubes.

    Stawberries: Wash berries. Remove stems.

    Grapes: Remove from stem. Wash.

    Watermelon: Cut fruit from rind. Cut melon into 1-inch cubes. Remove any seeds.

    Peach: Remove pit. Peel skin from fruit. Cut into quarters.

    Pear: Cut out core. Peel away skin. Cut into quarters.

3. Piece by piece, put the fruit on the wooden stick. Arrange the fruit in an attractive pattern.

Bonus Activity: How many different fruits can you name? Make a list including as many as possible. Check the grocery ads and markets for additional fruits. Have you tried all the fruits on your list? Mark an * beside those that you have not yet tasted.

© 1987 J. Weston Walch, Publisher   *62 Easy and Delicious Cooking Activities*

NAME _____ DATE _____

Ham Roll-Up (SERVINGS: 1)

Use frozen rolls to make these elegant sandwiches.

Ingredients: **Utensils:**

   1 frozen refrigerator crescent roll   knife
   1 slice ham   baking pan
   1 slice American cheese
   1 teaspoon mustard

Directions:

1. Preheat oven to 400° (or as directed on package).
2. Spread out refrigerator biscuit into triangle shape.
3. Spread with mustard.
4. Lay ham on biscuit.
5. Lay cheese on ham.
6. Starting at wide side of triangle, roll biscuit, ham and cheese together.
7. Shape into crescent.
8. Bake 12 to 15 minutes or until lightly browned.

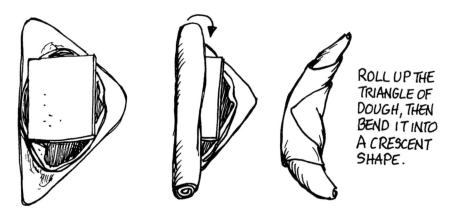

ROLL UP THE TRIANGLE OF DOUGH, THEN BEND IT INTO A CRESCENT SHAPE.

Bonus Activity: Refrigerator biscuits are quick and easy, but don't be limited by what the can tells you to do! List what you can do to make refrigerator biscuits more interesting. What fillings might you add? Could you cut them to make smaller appetizers? How many variations can you list?

© 1987 J. Weston Walch, Publisher   62 *Easy and Delicious Cooking Activities*

Muffin Sampler (SERVINGS: 4)

There's no limit to the variety of muffins you can make!

Ingredients for Basic Muffin Recipe:

- 1 small egg
- 2 tablespoons salad oil
- ¼ cup milk
- ¾ cup flour
- ¼ cup sugar
- 1 teaspoon baking powder
- ⅛ teaspoon salt

Utensils:

- 2 small bowls
- spoon for mixing
- measuring cup
- measuring spoons
- muffin tin
- paper liners for muffin cups
- wire cooling rack

Directions:

1. Preheat oven to 400°.
2. Break egg into bowl.
3. Stir in oil.
4. Stir in milk.
5. Combine flour, sugar, baking powder, and salt in separate bowl.
6. Add liquid ingredients to dry ingredients and mix just until flour is moistened. Batter should be lumpy.
7. Put paper liners in 4 muffin cups.
8. Fill cups ⅔ full.
9. Bake 20 minutes or until golden brown.
10. Cool muffins on rack.

(Continued on next sheet.)

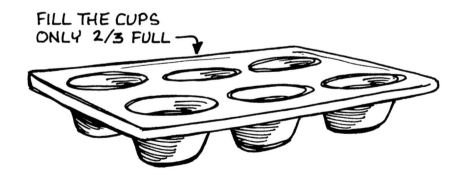

FILL THE CUPS ONLY 2/3 FULL

NAME _____ DATE _____

Muffin Sampler (continued)

Apple Muffins

Extra ingredients: 1 apple
1 teaspoon cinnamon, divided
2 tablespoons brown sugar

Extra utensils: small bowl

Directions:
- a. Do steps 1, 2, 3, and 4.
- b. Peel apple, remove core, and cut into small pieces. Add apple to liquid ingredients.
- c. Do step 5. Also add ½ teaspoon cinnamon to dry ingredients.
- d. Do steps 6, 7, and 8.
- e. In small bowl, combine brown sugar and ½ teaspoon cinnamon. Sprinkle crumb mixture over muffins.
- f. Finish with steps 9 and 10.

Blueberry Muffins

Extra ingredients: ½ cup fresh blueberries
- a. Do steps, 1, 2, 3, 4, and 5.
- b. Wash blueberries. Stir into flour mixture.
- c. Continue with steps 6, 7, 8, 9, and 10.

Orange Muffins

Extra ingredients: 1 orange

Extra utensils: juicer
grater

Directions:
- a. Grate rind from orange to make 2 teaspoons.
- b. Squeeze orange to make ¼ cup juice.
- c. Do steps, 1, 2, and 3.
- d. In step 4, add ¼ cup orange juice instead of milk.
- e. Do step 5, also adding grated peel.
- f. Continue with steps 6, 7, 8, 9, and 10.

(Continued on next sheet.)

© 1987 J. Weston Walch, Publisher   *62 Easy and Delicious Cooking Activities*

NAME _____ DATE _____

Muffin Sampler (continued)

Surprise Muffins

Extra ingredients: 4 teaspoons jelly or jam

Extra utensils: teaspoon

Directions:
- a. Do steps 1, 2, 3, 4, 5, 6, and 7.
- b. Fill muffin cups half full.
- c. Drop 1 teaspoon jelly in center of each muffin.
- d. Add more batter to fill cups 2/3 full.
- e. Continue with steps 9 and 10.

Bonus Activity What kind of muffins would you like to create? Think about your favorite fruit or flavor that might be a good addition to a muffin. How will you adapt the basic recipe for your variation? Will you make substitutions in the basic recipe? Will you add something to the finished batter? Will you sprinkle something on the muffins in the cups just before baking? Write out the recipe for your muffin variation.

NAME _____ DATE _____

Omelet (SERVINGS: 1)

Any number of leftovers can be the filling for your omelet.

Ingredients:

2 eggs
2 teaspoons water
1 tablespoon butter or margarine
2 to 3 tablespoons of filling—choose from:
    cheese, tomato, meat (cooked), green pepper, onion, other vegetables
salt
pepper
sprig of parsley

Utensils:

small bowl
measuring spoons
fork for mixing
10-inch skillet
spatula
luncheon plate
fork

Directions:

FOLD ONE HALF OVER TO COVER FILLING

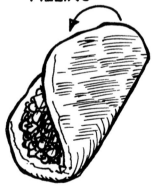

1. Break eggs into a small bowl.
2. Add water.
3. Whip with a fork.
4. Select fillings and prepare them for the omelet. Total amount of fillings shouldn't be more than 2 to 3 tablespoons.
5. Melt butter in the skillet.
6. Pour egg into the pan.
7. When egg begins to set, add the filling on half the pan.
8. Sprinkle with salt and pepper.
9. When egg is lightly browned, fold half over filling.
10. Slide onto plate.
11. Garnish with parsley and serve hot.

Bonus Activity: Check a recipe book to see what omelet recipes are included. How are the recipes similar? How are they different? Do they all prepare the eggs in the same way before cooking? What different fillings are used? Which recipes are easier to make? Which recipes are more difficult?

© 1987 J. Weston Walch, Publisher   *62 Easy and Delicious Cooking Activities*

NAME _____ DATE _____

Peanut Butter Soup (SERVINGS: 4)

Everyone loves peanut butter sandwiches; now try peanut butter soup.

Ingredients:

1 small onion
¼ cup butter or margarine
1 tablespoon flour
½ cup peanut butter
2 cups water
2 chicken bouillon cubes
salt
pepper
½ cup light cream
2 tablespoons peanuts

Utensils:

paring knife
chopping board
medium-sized saucepan
measuring spoons
measuring cups
strainer
nut chopper
tea kettle
medium-sized bowl
wooden spoon
soup ladle

4 small soup bowls
4 soupspoons

Directions:

_____   1. Peel and chop onion very fine.

_____   2. Melt butter in saucepan over low flame.

_____   3. Add the onion and simmer until the onion is light gold, but not brown. Remove from heat.

(Continued on next sheet.)

STRAIN SOUP INTO A BOWL, THEN POUR IT BACK INTO THE SAUCEPAN

© 1987 J. Weston Walch, Publisher   62 Easy and Delicious Cooking Activities

NAME _____ DATE _____

Peanut Butter Soup (continued)

_____ 4. With wooden spoon, stir in flour until smooth and no lumps remain.

_____ 5. Add peanut butter, stirring again until smooth. Set mixture aside.

_____ 6. Heat water in a tea kettle.

_____ 7. Put boullion cubes in medium-sized bowl.

_____ 8. Add 2 cups boiling water. Mix until cubes dissolve.

_____ 9. Return peanut butter mixture to heat.

_____ 10. Gradually add boullion mixture to peanut butter mixture, stirring all the time.

_____ 11. Add salt and pepper to taste.

_____ 12. Continue to cook and stir until mixture thickens.

_____ 13. Turn flame to low, stirring only occasionally. Allow the soup to simmer for 10 minutes.

_____ 14. Set strainer in a bowl. Pour soup through strainer into bowl. Then pour soup back into saucepan.

_____ 15. Add cream. Stir well. Return to flame and reheat.

_____ 16. Ladle into 4 bowls.

_____ 17. Chop peanuts into fine pieces and sprinkle over each portion.

Bonus Activity: George Washington Carver is well known for his work developing the peanut. Use an encyclopedia to learn more about Mr. Carver. When did he live? What did he do during his life? What uses did he discover for the peanut? Why was his work important?

© 1987 J. Weston Walch, Publisher   62 *Easy and Delicious Cooking Activities*

DATE _____

Peanut Crunchies (SERVINGS: 4)

This sweet nutty snack will be a favorite.

Ingredients:

    ½-pound unsalted peanuts in the shell
    ⅓ cup water
    ⅓ cup sugar
    ½ teaspoon cinnamon

Utensils:

    food chopper
    small bowl
    measuring cup
    measuring spoons
    heavy-bottomed saucepan
    wooden spoon
    waxed paper

Directions:

_____ 1. Shell the peanuts to make 1 cup of nut meats.

_____ 2. Chop the peanuts until fine.

_____ 3. Combine the water and sugar in the saucepan.

_____ 4. Over low heat, stir the water and sugar until the sugar dissolves.

_____ 5. Add the peanuts and cinnamon.

_____ 6. Continue stirring for about 3 minutes until the sugar turns light brown. Be careful that the mixture doesn't burn.

_____ 7. Remove the pan from the heat and let cool about 10 minutes, until cool enough to handle but still soft.

_____ 8. Pick up bits of the mixture and shape into 1-inch balls. Mixture will make about 8 balls. Place on waxed paper until set.

Bonus Activity: In addition to the peanut, how many other nuts can you list? How many of these are available in your store? What nuts are the most expensive? Which ones are the least expensive? What is the most expensive way to buy nuts? What is the least expensive?

NAME _____ DATE _____

Pretzels (SERVINGS: 4)

Germans were the first to make these salted bread shapes.

Ingredients:

- ¾ cup lukewarm water
- 1½ teaspoons yeast
- 2 cups (approximately) flour
- 1½ teaspoons sugar
- margarine to grease baking sheet
- egg
- water
- coarse salt

Utensils:

- mixing bowl
- measuring cup
- measuring spoons
- mixing spoon
- baking sheet
- small bowl
- pastry brush
- spatula
- wire cooling rack

Directions:

_____ 1. Preheat oven to 425°.

_____ 2. Pour the lukewarm water into the mixing bowl. Mix in the sugar.

_____ 3. Sprinkle the yeast on the water. Let it set about 5 minutes until bubbly.

_____ 4. Add 1½ cups flour to the yeast mixture. Stir until the ingredients are blended and form a ball.

_____ 5. Place the dough on a lightly floured surface.

_____ 6. Dust your hands with flour and knead dough.
   a. Use heels of your hands to push dough away.
   b. Turn the dough ¼ of the way around.
   c. Fold the dough over toward you.
   d. Push again with heels of your hands.

(Continued on next sheet.)

KNEADING THE DOUGH

TURN ¼ AROUND
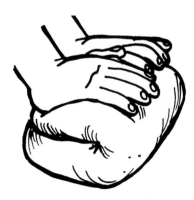

© 1987 J. Weston Walch, Publisher   62 *Easy and Delicious Cooking Activities*

NAME _____ DATE _____

Pretzels (continued)

_____ 7. Knead in remainder of flour if needed. After about 5 minutes, the dough should be smooth and not sticky.

_____ 8. Divide the dough into 4 pieces.

_____ 9. Roll each piece into a long snake about ½ inch thick and 15 inches long. Shape the dough into a pretzel as shown in the diagram.

_____ 10. Grease baking sheet. Place pretzels on the baking sheet, allowing several inches of space between pretzels.

_____ 11. Combine the egg with 1 tablespoon of water. Paint mixture on each pretzel. Sprinkle with coarse salt.

_____ 12. Bake for 10 minutes. Remove from oven. Cool on wire rack.

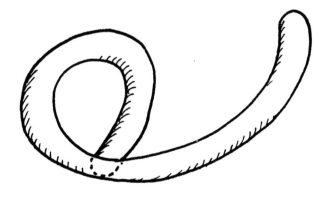

PRESS TOGETHER

Bonus Activity: Many of the foods we enjoy have their origins in other cultures. How many "foreign" dishes can you list? Beside each food, write the name of the country where it originated.

NAME _____ DATE _____

Rice Variations (SERVINGS: 1)

Have your rice any way you like it!

Ingredients:

    ¼ cup regular white rice
    ½ cup water
    ¼ teaspoon salt

Utensils:

    small saucepan with cover
    measuring cup
    measuring spoons
    wooden spoon
    fork

Directions:

1. Combine rice, water, and salt in saucepan.
2. Heat to boiling, stirring once or twice.
3. Reduce heat to simmer. Cover pan tightly and cook 14 minutes. Do not lift cover or stir.
4. Remove pan from heat.
5. Fluff rice lightly with fork.
6. Cover and let steam 5 minutes longer.

Beefy Rice

Extra ingredients: 1 beef boullion cube

Directions:
    a. In step 1, add boullion cube to water.
    b. Continue with steps, 2, 3, 4, 5, and 6.

Spanish Rice

Extra ingredients: 1 link sweet sausage
    ¼ cup spaghetti sauce

Extra utensils: small skillet
    paper towel

Directions:
    a. Do steps 1, 2, 3, 4, 5, and 6.
    b. Cook sausage in skillet until brown. Drain on paper towel. Crumble into small pieces.
    c. Add sausage and spaghetti sauce to cooked rice.

(Continued on next sheet.)

© 1987 J. Weston Walch, Publisher

NAME _____ DATE _____

Rice Variations (continued)

Hawaiian Rice

Extra ingredients: ¼ cup pineapple juice
¼ cup chopped ham

Directions:
a. In step 1, reduce water to ¼ cup and add ¼ cup pineapple juice.
b. Continue with steps 2, 3, 4, 5, and 6.
c. Add ham to cooked rice.

Almond Rice

Extra ingredients: 2 tablespoons slivered almonds
1 teaspoon butter or margarine

Extra Utensils: small skillet

Directions:
a. Do steps 1, 2, 3, 4, 5, and 6.
b. Melt butter in saucepan.
c. Brown almonds in butter, stirring constantly.
d. Mix almonds into cooked rice.

Curried Rice

Extra ingredients: chicken boullion cube
½ teaspoon curry powder
½ apple

Extra utensils: paring knife

Directions:
a. Peel, core, and chop apple.
b. In step 1, also add chicken boullion cube, curry powder, and apple to saucepan.
c. Continue with steps 2, 3, 4, 5, and 6.

(Continued on next sheet.)

© 1987 J. Weston Walch, Publisher   62 *Easy and Delicious Cooking Activities*

Rice Variations (continued)

Fried Rice

Extra ingredients: 1 green onion
1 small egg, beaten
1 teaspoon soy sauce
1 teaspoon butter

Extra Utensils: small skillet
small bowl
paring knife
chopping board

Directions:
a. Cook rice, following steps 1, 2, 3, 4, 5, and 6.
b. Chop green onions into small pieces.
c. Break egg into bowl and beat lightly.
d. Melt butter in skillet.
e. Saute green onion in butter.
f. Add cooked rice and soy sauce.
g. Pour egg over rice.
h. Stir lightly 2 to 3 minutes until all ingredients are cooked.

Bonus Activity: How would you like your rice? Would you cook it in something other than plain water? Would you add other items to the rice after it has cooked? Write a recipe for rice the way you would like it. Be sure to include a name for your rice dish.

Sausage and Pepper Hero (SERVINGS: 12)

Make this sandwich to feed the whole gang!

Ingredients:

two 15-inch loaves Italian bread
2 pounds sweet Italian sausage lengths
3 large green peppers
2 large onions
1 can (29 ounces) crushed tomatoes
1 teaspoon salt
½ teaspoon dried basil
½ teaspoon dried oregano
¼ teaspoon black pepper
8 ounces mozzarella cheese

Utensils:

bread knife
aluminum foil
paring knife
chopping board
Dutch oven
slotted spoon
can or container for grease
paper towel
small bowl
can opener
measuring spoons
cheese grater
baking sheet

12 luncheon plates

Directions:

1. Preheat oven to 400°.
2. Split 2 loaves of bread almost through, lengthwise.
3. Wrap each loaf of bread in foil. Put in oven for 15 minutes to warm through.
4. Cut sausage into 1-inch pieces.
5. In Dutch oven, cook sausage over medium heat until browned.

(Continued on next sheet.)

PUT HALF OF THE SAUSAGE MIXTURE INTO EACH SPLIT LOAF, THEN REWRAP IN FOIL

© 1987 J. Weston Walch, Publisher

62 Easy and Delicious Cooking Activities

NAME _____ DATE _____

Sausage and Pepper Hero (continued)

_____ 6. Remove with slotted spoon. Drain sausage on paper towels.

_____ 7. Discard all but 2 tablespoons of drippings.

_____ 8. Wash green peppers. Remove seeds and slice into long strips.

_____ 9. Peel onions and slice.

_____ 10. Cook green peppers and onions in Dutch oven for 5 minutes. Stir occasionally.

_____ 11. In small bowl, combine tomatoes and herbs. Be sure tomatoes are thoroughly chopped.

_____ 12. Add tomato mixture and sausages to vegetables and cook 15 minutes. Stir as needed.

_____ 13. Shred cheese.

_____ 14. Open foil around bread. Place both loaves on baking sheet.

_____ 15. Fill each loaf with half the sausage mixture.

_____ 16. Sprinkle with grated cheese.

_____ 17. Bake 10 to 12 minutes until cheese is bubbly.

_____ 18. Cut each loaf into 6 servings.

Bonus Activity: Do some price comparisons to determine which is the best store to purchase ingredients for this dish. First make a list of the main ingredients. Check ads or the actual stores to find the cost for each of these items.

Is there one store that has the lowest price for every item? Are there different prices for any one item in the same store? Where do you think would be the best place to shop for ingredients for this recipe? Are there other factors than price to consider when deciding where to shop?

© 1987 J. Weston Walch, Publisher *62 Easy and Delicious Cooking Activities*

NAME _____ DATE _____

Scones & Strawberry Jam (SERVINGS: 4)

Scones with tea are a favorite treat for the English.

Ingredients:

    1 cup flour
    1½ teaspoons baking powder
    ¼ teaspoon salt
    1 tablespoon sugar
    2 tablespoons butter or margarine
    ¼ cup cream
    1 egg
    flour for rolling out dough
    sugar for top of scones
    8 to 10 strawberries (⅓
        of a 10-ounce package)
    ¼ cup sugar

Utensils:

    2 small bowls
    measuring spoons
    measuring cup
    spoon for mixing
    knife
    baking sheet
    spatula
    saucepan
    wire cooling rack
    wooden spoon

Directions:

_____	1. Preheat oven to 375°.
_____	2. Combine flour, baking powder, salt, and sugar in a bowl.
_____	3. Add butter. Use fingers to mix the butter with the dry ingredients.
_____	4. In a separate bowl, combine the egg and cream.
_____	5. Mix liquid into the dry ingredients.
_____	6. On a floured surface, pat dough into rectangle ¾-inch thick.
_____	7. Cut into 2 squares.
_____	8. Cut each square into 2 triangles.
_____	9. Put on baking sheet. Sprinkle with sugar.
_____	10. Bake 20 minutes or until lightly browned. Cool on wire rack.
_____	11. Put frozen strawberries in saucepan. Thaw over medium heat, stirring continuously.
_____	12. Bring to a boil.
_____	13. Add sugar. Keep boiling and stirring for 3 to 5 minutes until mixture thickens.
_____	14. Remove from heat. Skim off any foam or scum.
_____	15. Put in freezer 10 minutes to help it cool quickly. Serve on hot scones.

Bonus Activity: Ask your teacher for cards to play NUTRO.

© 1987 J. Weston Walch, Publisher   *62 Easy and Delicious Cooking Activities*

NAME _____ DATE _____

Snow Ice Cream (SERVINGS: 1)

A special treat when the snow flies!

Ingredients:

    2/3 cup milk
    1 egg
    2 tablespoons sugar
    1½ teaspoons vanilla
    snow (about 1 cup)

Utensils:

    small bowl
    whisk
    mixing spoon
    measuring cup
    measuring spoon

Directions:

1. Break egg into bowl. Use whisk to beat well.
2. Add sugar, milk, and vanilla. Mix well.
3. Fold in fresh, clean snow to desired consistency.
4. If snow is unavailable, finely crushed ice can be substituted.

Bonus Activity: New Englanders have "sugaring-off" parties after a new snow in the spring. It is at the time when sap is running in the maple trees. Some of the syrup is cooked extra thick and drizzled over pans of new snow for a special treat. See if you can find any more information about this part of New England's heritage.

© 1987 J. Weston Walch, Publisher   62 *Easy and Delicious Cooking Activities*

NAME _____ DATE _____

Stuffed Pasta Shells (SERVINGS: 4)

This is an unusual pasta variation.

Ingredients:

    8 jumbo macaroni shells
       (about 4 ounces)
    water for cooking shells
    ½ pound ricotta cheese
    2 ounces mozzarella cheese
    1 small egg
    2 saltine crackers
    ¾ teaspoon dried parsley
    ¼ teaspoon salt
    dash of black pepper
    1 cup meatless spaghetti sauce
    2 tablespoons grated Parmesan cheese

Utensils:

    small saucepan
    small bowl
    spoon for mixing
    slotted spoon
    baking dish
    cheese grater

    4 luncheon plates
    4 forks

Directions:

_____   1. Preheat oven to 375°.

_____   2. Half fill saucepan with water. Bring to a rolling boil.

_____   3. Add shells. Boil uncovered 12 to 15 minutes. Stir occasionally.

_____   4. Use slotted spoon to remove shells from water. Place in baking dish.

_____   5. Put ricotta cheese in bowl.

_____   6. Grate mozzarella cheese. Add to bowl.

_____   7. Add egg.

_____   8. Crumble crackers to small crumbs. Add.

_____   9. Add parsley, salt, and pepper. Mix thoroughly.

_____   10. Spoon filling into cooked shells.

_____   11. Cover shells with spaghetti sauce.

_____   12. Sprinkle Parmesan cheese over shells.

_____   13. Bake 15 to 20 minutes or until warmed through.

Bonus Activity: Make a list of your favorite dishes that include pasta. What different kinds of pasta do these recipes include? How many other varieties can you list?

© 1987 J. Weston Walch, Publisher   *62 Easy and Delicious Cooking Activities*

Stuffed Pita Pockets (SERVINGS: 4)

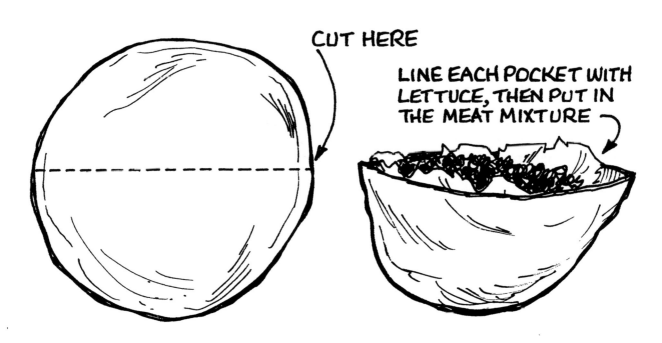

This recipe for a practical leak-proof sandwich is from Lebanon.

Ingredients:

    1 small onion
    1 tablespoon butter or margarine
    ½ pound ground beef
    ½ teaspoon salt
    ¼ teaspoon black pepper
    1 tablespoon chopped dill
    1 medium tomato
    2 pieces of pita bread
    4 lettuce leaves

Utensils:

    paring knife
    chopping board
    medium frying pan
    wooden spoon
    measuring spoons
    slotted spoon
    paper towel
    bread knife

Directions:

1. Use a paring knife to peel the onion. Chop the onion fine on a chopping board.
2. Melt the butter in the frying pan.
3. Sauté the onion in the butter for 5 minutes. Stir with a wooden spoon to keep it from burning.

(Continued on next sheet.)

© 1987 J. Weston Walch, Publisher   *62 Easy and Delicious Cooking Activities*

NAME _____ DATE _____

Stuffed Pita Pockets (continued)

_____ 4. Add the meat, salt, pepper, and dill. Mix well. Cook over medium heat, breaking the meat up with the spoon. Stir until the meat browns.

_____ 5. Cut the tomato into small pieces.

_____ 6. Stir the tomatoes into the meat mixture.

_____ 7. Use a slotted spoon to remove the meat mixture from the pan. Drain on a paper towel.

_____ 8. Slice both pita breads in half to make four pockets.

_____ 9. Line each pocket with a lettuce leaf.

_____ 10. Add a heaping spoonful of the meat and tomato mixture.

Bonus Activity: Bread comes in a wide variety of shapes and forms. How many can you list? How many different shapes can you list? What about different flavors—can you list a variety of flours that are used for bread? Check your local store to add to your list.

Sweet & Sour Meatballs (SERVINGS: 4)

One more of the 1,001 variations for hamburg.

Ingredients:

　　1 slice soft bread
　　¾-pound ground beef
　　½ teaspoon salt
　　1 egg
　　1 tablespoon oil
　　3 carrots
　　3 stalks celery
　　1 green pepper
　　2 tablespoons soy sauce
　　1 tablespoon cider vinegar
　　¼ teaspoon ground ginger
　　½ cup water
　　one 8-ounce can pineapple chunks
　　1 tablespoon cornstarch

Utensils:

　　medium bowl
　　wooden spoon
　　waxed paper
　　large skillet
　　paper towel
　　slotted spoon
　　vegetable parer
　　paring knife
　　chopping board
　　measuring spoon
　　measuring cup
　　small bowl
　　can opener
　　4 luncheon plates
　　4 forks

Directions:

_____   1. Break bread into small crumbs.
_____   2. Combine ground beef, bread crumbs, and salt in mixing bowl.
_____   3. Break egg into bowl. Mix all ingredients.
　　　　　　　　　　　 4. Form into 16 meatballs. Set on piece of waxed paper.

(Continued on next sheet.)

© 1987 J. Weston Walch, Publisher　　　　　　62 Easy and Delicious Cooking Activities

NAME _____ DATE _____

Sweet & Sour Meatballs (continued)

_____ 5. Heat oil in skillet.

_____ 6. Brown meatballs. Use slotted spoon to remove meatballs from pan. Drain on paper towel.

_____ 7. Pare carrots. Slice. Add to pan.

_____ 8. Wash celery. Slice and add to pan.

_____ 9. Add soy sauce, vinegar, ginger, and water to pan. Stir. Cover and simmer 5 minutes.

_____ 10. Wash pepper. Remove seeds. Cut into thin strips.

_____ 11. Drain pineapple juice into small bowl.

_____ 12. Add cornstarch to pineapple juice. Mix until well blended. Add to cooking mixture.

_____ 13. Add pineapple, green pepper, and meatballs.

_____ 14. Simmer 5 minutes longer.

Bonus Activity: Ground beef has certainly become one of the most versatile foods in the American diet. Whole cookbooks have been written with recipes for ground beef.

How many uses for ground beef can you list? This recipe makes one use. Now how many more . . .?

© 1987 J. Weston Walch, Publisher   *62 Easy and Delicious Cooking Activities*

Tomato Flower (SERVINGS: 1)

This salad is a good summer lunch.

Ingredients:

1 egg
water to cook egg
1 large tomato
½ stalk of celery
1 tablespoon mayonnaise
½ teaspoon minced onion
paprika

Utensils:

small saucepan
small bowl
fork
measuring spoon
paring knife
cutting board
luncheon plate
fork

Directions:

1. Put egg in saucepan.
2. Cover with cold water and bring water to a boil.
3. Reduce heat and cook 11 minutes.
4. When cooked, drain hot water. Cover egg with cold water. Continue to replace water with cold water until egg is cooled.

(Continued on next sheet.)

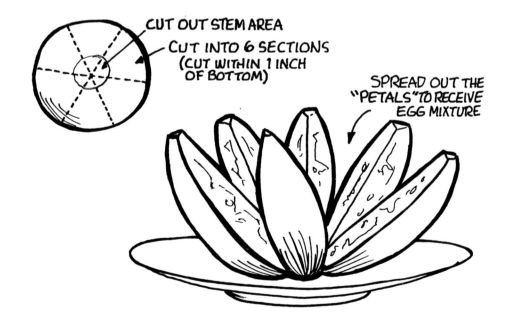

CUT OUT STEM AREA
CUT INTO 6 SECTIONS (CUT WITHIN 1 INCH OF BOTTOM)
SPREAD OUT THE "PETALS" TO RECEIVE EGG MIXTURE

NAME _____ DATE _____

Tomato Flower (continued)

5. Cut stem end off tomato.
6. Cut tomato into sixths, cutting to within 1 inch of the bottom. Put on luncheon plate.
7. Carefully spread out sections, forming a flower.
8. Peel egg. Put it in the small bowl.
9. Wash celery. Chop very fine. Add to bowl with egg.
10. Add mayonnaise and minced onion. Mix well.
11. Fill tomato with egg salad.
12. Sprinkle with paprika.

Bonus Activity: This recipe uses the tomato as a serving dish for other food. People eat dish and all.
What other foods can be used in this way? What fillings would be appropriate for each? If you need help, consult a cookbook.

© 1987 J. Weston Walch, Publisher

NAME _____ DATE _____

Tomato Soup (SERVINGS: 1)

This soup is fun to make in the fall when fresh tomatoes are plentiful.

Ingredients:

    1 large ripe tomato
    1 teaspoon butter or margarine
    ½ teaspoon granulated chicken
       boullion
    ½ cup water
    ¼ cup milk or cream
    salt
    black pepper
    celery leaves

Utensils:

    small saucepan
    paring knife
    wooden spoon
    measuring spoons
    measuring cup
    fork
    blender
    mug
    soupspoon

Directions:

1. Peel the tomato. A quick way to do this is to place the tomato in very hot water for 1 minute. Use a fork to transfer the tomato to cold water. The skin will come off easily.
2. Use a paring knife to cut the tomato into small pieces.
3. Melt the butter in the saucepan.
4. Sauté the tomato in the butter until it is tender.
5. Add boullion and ½ cup hot water. Simmer for 15 minutes.
6. Put the mixture in a food blender and puree. Be sure to start blender on the very lowest setting and hold cover on securely.
7. Return soup to the saucepan.
8. Add milk or cream. Stir and heat through.
9. Pour into mug to serve.
10. Garnish with celery leaf.

Bonus Activity: Consult recipe books to find 10 recipes that call for tomatoes. How are tomatoes used in each of these recipes? Are the tomatoes essential ingredients or could they be left out? Are there any foods that could be substituted for tomatoes in any of the recipes?

© 1987 J. Weston Walch, Publisher   *62 Easy and Delicious Cooking Activities*

NAME _____ DATE _____

Tossed Salad (SERVINGS: 12)

Your own preferences can determine the recipe for tossed salad.

Ingredients:

    1 head lettuce
    2 large tomatoes
    1 large purple onion
    2 carrots
    1 green pepper
    ½-pound fresh mushrooms
    3 stalks celery
    1 small cucumber
    1 stalk broccoli
    ½ small head of cauliflower
    6 to 8 radishes
    1 can tomato soup
    ¼ cup sugar
    ⅓ cup salad oil
    ⅓ cup cider vinegar
    1 teaspoon garlic powder
    1 teaspoon celery salt

Utensils:

    large salad bowl
    salad fork and spoon
    paring knife
    cutting board
    vegetable parer
    small bowl
    can opener
    spoon for mixing
    measuring cup
    measuring spoon

    12 salad plates
    12 forks

Directions:

_____ 1. Wash lettuce. Tear into bite-sized pieces.

_____ 2. Wash tomatoes. Remove cores. Cut into bite-sized pieces.

_____ 3. Peel onion. Slice. Separate each slice into rings.

_____ 4. Pare carrots. Cut into thin slices.

_____ 5. Remove core from green pepper. Wash and cut into small pieces.

                                  6. Wash mushrooms. Slice.

_____ 7. Wash celery. Trim ends from celery. Cut into slices.

_____ 8. Peel cucumber. Cut into quarters lengthwise. Cut quarters into
_____   small bite-sized pieces.

Bonus Activity: There are several types of lettuce. Check at the supermarket to find out how many different types of lettuce are sold. What are the features of each kind? Which would you prefer in a tossed salad?

    Check the other ingredients called for in the salad. Is there more than one type of cucumber? How about onions? What other vegetables come in a variety of types?

© 1987 J. Weston Walch, Publisher   *62 Easy and Delicious Cooking Activities*

NAME _____ DATE _____

Tuna Cheesie (SERVINGS: 1)

Try this variation on the favorite tuna sandwich!

Ingredients

1 ounce tuna
   (about 1/6 of a 6½-ounce can)
¼ small onion
¼ stick celery
1 teaspoon mayonnaise
salt
pepper
½ English muffin
1 slice tomato
1 slice American cheese

Utensils:

paring knife
cutting board
small mixing bowl
measuring spoons
fork for mixing
toaster
broiler pan

Directions:

1. Turn oven temperature to broil.
2. Peel onion and chop very fine.
3. Chop celery until fine.
4. Combine tuna, onion, and celery in small bowl.
5. Sprinkle with salt and pepper.
6. Add mayonnaise and mix all ingredients together.
7. Toast English muffin half.
8. Spread tuna mixture on muffin.
9. Place tomato slice on tuna.
10. Top with cheese slice trimmed to fit.
11. Put on the pan. Broil 5 inches from heat for 3 to 5 minutes or until cheese is melted and golden brown.

Bonus Activity: This recipe does not make a complete meal. What is missing to make it a balanced meal? Check a recipe book to find a new and interesting recipe that could be served with this dish.

© 1987 J. Weston Walch, Publisher   62 *Easy and Delicious Cooking Activities*

NAME _____ DATE _____

Vegetable Bouquet (SERVINGS: 1)

This bouquet will add a decorative touch to any buffet table.

Ingredients:

1 celery stalk
1 carrot
3 to 4 radishes
3 to 4 cherry tomatoes
1 tablespoon whipped cream cheese
1 orange

Utensils:

paring knife
vegetable peeler
toothpicks
dish of ice water
saucer or basket

Directions:

1. Celery curls: wash celery; cut stalk into 3-inch lengths; slit into narrow strips at both ends; soak in ice water until ends curl.

2. Radish roses: wash radishes; cut off root end; cut "petals" around radish from root end almost to stem end; place "roses" in ice water to "blossom."

(Continued on next sheet.)

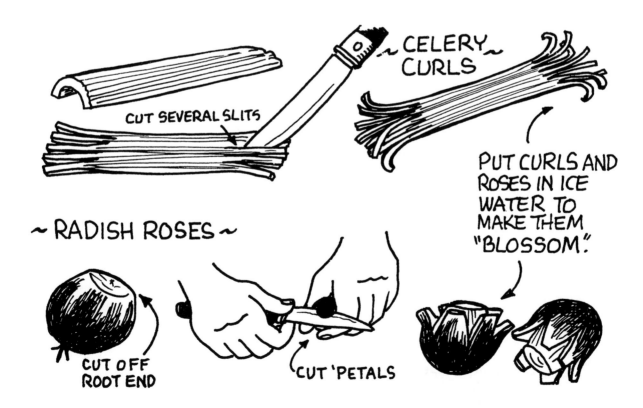

© 1987 J. Weston Walch, Publisher   62 Easy and Delicious Cooking Activities

Vegetable Bouquet (continued)

3. Carrot daises: peel carrot; cut 5 or 6 slices from widest end; use knife to cut petal pattern.
4. Carrot curls: use peeler to slice thin lengths of the carrot; roll carrot slices around finger; hold in shape with toothpick.
5. Tomato flowers: cut core out of tiny tomatoes; stuff with cream cheese.
6. Assemble bouquet: cut end off orange to make a flat area so it will stay in place; put orange on saucer or in decorative basket; use toothpicks to attach the flowers to the orange.

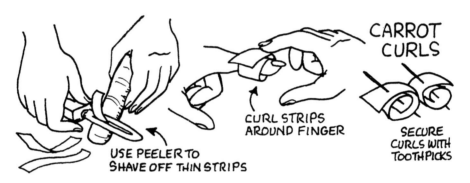

CARROT CURLS

CURL STRIPS AROUND FINGER

SECURE CURLS WITH TOOTHPICKS

USE PEELER TO SHAVE OFF THIN STRIPS

CARROT DAISIES

CUT "PETALS" ON SECTIONS OF CARROT AS IT IS DONE FOR RADISH ROSES

TOMATO FLOWERS

CUT CORES OUT OF CHERRY TOMATOES AND FILL WITH CREAM CHEESE

Bonus Activity: What other foods could be used to make flowers? How would they be cut to resemble flowers? Do not limit yourself to just vegetables. Try fruits.

© 1987 J. Weston Walch, Publisher   62 *Easy and Delicious Cooking Activities*

NAME _____ DATE _____

Vegetable Sampler (SERVINGS: 4)

Try these ideas to make ordinary vegetables more interesting.

Green Beans Almandine

1 pound fresh green beans
boiling water
½ teaspoon salt
2 tablespoons butter
¼ cup sliced almonds

saucepan with cover
small skillet
wooden spoon
colander

serving dish
serving spoon

1. Rinse beans. Use your fingers to snap the ends off the beans.
2. Put beans and salt in pan. Add enough water to cover the beans.
3. Cover saucepan. Simmer 10 to 12 minutes over medium heat.
4. Melt butter in the skillet.
5. Add almonds. Stir to coat with butter.
6. Cook over low heat until brown and toasty, stirring continuously.
7. Drain cooked beans in colander.
8. Place beans in serving dish. Add almonds and toss gently.

Orange Juice Carrots

1 orange (for 2 teaspoons grated peel)
⅔ cup orange juice
¼ cup butter
2 tablespooons brown sugar
½ teaspoon salt
⅛ teaspoon ground nutmeg
1 pound carrots

saucepan with cover
grater
vegetable parer
measuring spooons
paring knive
chopping board
wooden spoon

serving dish
serving spoon

1. Wash orange. Grate enough peel to make 2 teaspoons.
2. Pare carrots. Slice thin.
3. Mix all ingredients except carrots in the saucepan. Bring to a boil over medium high heat.
4. Add carrots. Reduce heat to medium. Cover and simmer 5 minutes.
5. Uncover. Cook 15 minutes longer until carrots are tender and just a small amount of sauce remains.
6. Put in serving dish.

(Continued on next sheet.)

© 1987 J. Weston Walch, Publisher   62 Easy and Delicious Cooking Activities

NAME _____ DATE _____

Vegetable Sampler (continued)

Sesame Corn

3 ears fresh corn
3 tablespoons butter
1 clove garlic
¼ green pepper
2 tablespoons sesame seeds
½ teaspoon salt
¼ teaspoon basil
⅛ teaspoon black pepper

paring knife
cutting board
measuring cup
garlic press
saucepan with cover
wooden spoon

serving dish
serving spoon

1. Husk corn and remove silk. Cut enough kernels from ears to measure 1½ cups.
2. Put butter in saucepan. Melt.
3. Crush garlic in press. Add to saucepan.
4. Chop green pepper. Add to saucepan.
5. Add sesame seeds, salt, basil, and black pepper. Stir all together.
6. Add corn. Mix ingredients.
7. Cover. Cook over low heat 15 minutes or until corn is tender.
8. Put in serving dish.

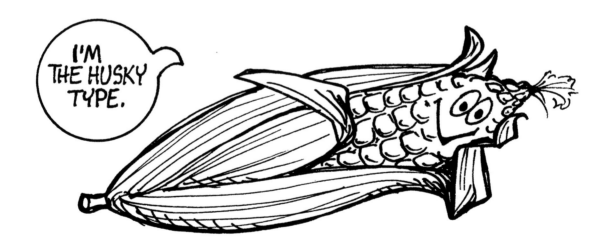

Bonus Activity: Compare fresh vegetables with canned vegetables and frozen vegetables. How do they compare in cost? How do they compare in nutrition?

Consult a cookbook or talk with someone who does canning and freezing to find out what is involved in each process.

What are the advantages and disadvantages of using each of the three kinds of vegetables . . . fresh, frozen, and canned?

© 1987 J. Weston Walch, Publisher   *62 Easy and Delicious Cooking Activities*

NAME _____ DATE _____

Waldorf Salad (SERVINGS: 1)

This salad takes its name from the famous hotel where it was first served.

Ingredients:

1 medium, bright red apple
1 stalk celery
nutmeats of 3 to 4 walnuts
2 tablespoons raisins
2 to 3 tablespoons mayonnaise or salad dressing

Utensils:

paring knife
chopping board
measuring spoons
small bowl
mixing spoon

Directions:

1. Rinse the apple. Remove core. Cut into 4 sections. Dice each quarter of the apple and place in bowl.
2. Wash celery. Remove leaves. Slice the celery stalk. Add to bowl.
3. Break nutmeats into coarse pieces. Add to bowl.
4. Add raisins.
5. Gently mix in desired amount of mayonnaise.
6. Keep chilled until serving time.

Bonus Activity: What is the definition of a salad? Don't look in a dictionary to find the answer. Think about what you know about salads or look at a variety of salad recipes. What do they all have in common? What is it about each of them that makes them a "salad"? Write a short definition that describes only salad.

© 1987 J. Weston Walch, Publisher *62 Easy and Delicious Cooking Activities*

NAME _____ DATE _____

Walnut Chicken & Rice (SERVINGS: 4)

Try wok cooking with this crunchy chicken recipe.

Ingredients:

- 1 boneless chicken breast
- ½ teaspoon ground ginger
- 4 tablespoons salad oil (divided)
- 2 tablespoons soy sauce
- 1 tablespoon cornstarch
- 1 medium onion
- 1 red bell pepper
- 1 stalk broccoli
- 1 chicken boullion cube
- ½ cup water
- ½ cup walnuts
- ⅔ cup rice
- 1 ⅓ cups water
- ½ teaspoon salt

Utensils:

- paring knife
- chopping board
- small bowl
- measuring spoons
- spoon for mixing
- saucepan with cover
- wooden spoon
- fork
- wok or large skillet
- 4 luncheon plates
- 4 forks

Directions:

_____ 1. Remove skin from chicken. Cut into 1-inch pieces.

_____ 2. Mix together ginger, soy sauce, cornstarch, and 1 tablespoon salad oil.

_____ 3. Stir in chicken to coat. Set aside.

_____ 4. Combine rice, 1 ⅓ cups water, and ½ teaspoon salt in saucepan. Heat to boiling, stirring once or twice.

_____ 5. Reduce heat to simmer. Cover tightly and cook 14 minutes.

(Continued on next sheet.)

WOK

© 1987 J. Weston Walch, Publisher   *62 Easy and Delicious Cooking Activities*

NAME _____ DATE _____

Walnut Chicken & Rice (continued)

_____ 6. While rice is cooking, peel onion. Cut in half. Slice each half.

_____ 7. Wash red pepper. Remove seeds. Cut into 1-inch pieces.

_____ 8. Wash broccoli. Cut into 1-inch pieces.

_____ 9. Remove rice from heat. Fluff lightly with fork. Cover and let steam 5 more minutes.

_____ 10. Heat 3 tablespoons oil in wok or skillet.

_____ 11. Stir fry chicken over medium heat until no longer pink. Remove from pan.

_____ 12. Stir fry onion and red pepper in skillet until onion is tender.

_____ 13. Add broccoli; stir fry until tender.

_____ 14. Add boullion cube and ½ cup water.

_____ 15. Stir in cooked chicken.

_____ 16. Cook, stirring constantly until mixture thickens.

_____ 17. Coarsely chop walnuts. Add to mixture.

_____ 18. Put rice on plates.

_____ 19. Serve chicken/vegetable mixture over rice.

Bonus Activity: The wok is an oriental cooking pan. Look in a Chinese cookbook or other resource to find out more about the wok. How would you describe the shape? What is the origin of this cooking pan? What are the advantages of cooking in this kind of pan? What type of recipes work well in a wok?

© 1987 J. Weston Walch, Publisher   *62 Easy and Delicious Cooking Activities*

Welsh Rarebit (SERVINGS: 1)

If you like cheese, you'll love this simple-to-make meal!

Ingredients:

    1 tablespoon butter or margarine
    1 tablespoon flour
    pinch of dry mustard
    salt
    pepper
    Worcestershire sauce
    ⅓ cup milk
    ½ cup shredded cheddar cheese (about 2 ounces)
    1 slice bread
    paprika

Utensils:

    small saucepan
    wooden spoon
    measuring spoons
    measuring cup
    cheese grater
    toaster
    knife
    luncheon plate
    fork

Directions:

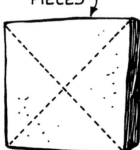

CUT TOAST INTO FOUR TRIANGULAR PIECES

1. Grate enough cheese to measure ½ cup. Set aside.
2. Melt butter in saucepan over low heat.
3. Remove from heat. Stir in flour and a pinch of dry mustard. Add a dash each of salt, pepper, and Worcestershire sauce.
4. Add small amount of milk.
5. Return to heat and stir constantly until mixture is smooth and bubbly.
6. Gradually add rest of milk. Continue stirring.
7. Heat to boiling. Stir 1 minute.
8. Add cheese. Stir and heat until melted. Remove from heat.
9. Toast slice of bread. Cut into 4 triangular pieces and put on plate.
10. Serve cheese mixture over toast.
11. Sprinkle with paprika for garnish.

Bonus Activity: This recipe starts with a white sauce. Check in a recipe book to find other recipes that start with a white sauce.